Pyrrhonism

dysphoria

nimiety ?
fainient ?
otoise ?

copula
metaphor for
the Holy Ghost

pucilanimous ?

God-Adam Theory
Brig. Young stressed
Joseph Fielding Smith denounced
in Doctrines of Salvation

pg 120
superannuated
thurification

He uses big words—
some, like those above,
I had to look up.

Spiritual Vision
של הכהן גדול

David B. Cohen, M.D.

Irving H. Cohen, D.D.S.

Published and Distributed by:

Granite Publishing and Distribution, LLC
868 North 1430 West
Orem, Utah 84057
(801) 229-9023 • Toll Free (800) 574-5779
Fax (801) 229-1924

Glyphic & Text Layout by
Design to Print, L.L.C., St. George, Utah

Cover Design by Rhett Nielson

Library of Congress Control Number: 2003110254
ISBN: 1-932280-20-0

First Printing, August 2003

Printed in the United States of America

10 9 8 7 6 5 4 3 2 1

Dedicatory Tribute

That the authors may turn their hearts to their fathers and the promises made to their fathers, this book is dedicated to our Uncle Moses and his brother Aaron, and all of his literal descendants including: Eleazar, Phineas, Ahimelech, Abiathar, Zadok, Jeremiah, Ezekial, Ezra, Zechariah, the Maccabees, Zacharias, John the Baptist, Rabbi Uri Tzvi Sr. (buried at the Mount of Olives), Rabbi David Cohen Sr. (buried in the land of Joseph), and all the other *Cohen Gadols** who have used or have had the legal right to use the Urim and Thummim to know the mysteries of God. Figuratively speaking, may the rod of Aaron contained in the Ark of the Covenant blossom forth once again.

---

* *Cohen Gadol* is Hebrew for "high priest"

Hebraic Glyphic
of the
Seventh Seal

There is more to wo than woe

Explanation of the Hebraic Glyphic

The spiritual eyes abide in the heart and are the windows of the soul and the light of the body (Matt. 6:22). The light scintillating from the eyes comes from the Spirit of God like a fire burning. The Urim and Thummim are the consummate symbols of spiritual vision, for they were placed over the auricles of the heart by the oracle wearing them (Ex. 28:30). The eyelid fissures are shaped like two almonds, a symbol of the watchfulness and vigilance of the spiritual eyes (see p. 107). As the physical heart is blood red, so is faith, for the ultimate manifestation of faith is the spilling of one's blood on the altar for the Messiah. In the end, love is also crimson, since *"Greater love hath no man than this, that a man lay down his life for his friends"* (John 15:13). The Star of David betokens the magnetism of the priesthood from the heavens above and the earth beneath. The Star of David may also be a two-dimensional depiction of the Urim and Thummim, which work together prismatically to put light traveling in *straight paths* into *"one eternal round"* (Alma 37:12; D&C 3:2). The ‎ו (o) and the ‎ו (u) are tokens of the Godhead. The sixth letter *vav* was chosen by the Godhead because They created man on the sixth day, and the *vav* resembles a human chromosome (‎ו); and also a nail. Moreover, the angle in the *vav* is the same angle that light makes as it passes through the Urim and Thummim. Nevertheless, it is only the *dagesh* directly above or in the middle that makes the *vav* holy. *Menorah* in Hebrew means "from the light of Jehovah," and was the only source of light in the Tabernacle and Solomon's temple as a similitude of the Messiah being the light and life of the world. The seven golden candlesticks not only represent the seven days of creation and the seven seals, but also the holy candelabrum that served as background to the Lord when He appeared to John the Revelator (Rev 1:13). The golden menorah burning up towards God could also represent a mouth speaking to God, which in Hebrew is *pe le El* (פה ל אל).

Prayer of the Cohens*

(Numbers 6:24-26)

The Lord bless thee and keep thee:

יברכך יהוה וישמרך

The Lord make His face shine upon

thee, and be gracious unto thee:

יאר יהוה פניו אליך ויחנך

The Lord lift up His countenance upon

thee, and give thee peace.

ישא יהוה פניו אליך וישם לך שלום

"And they [the Cohens] shall put my name upon the

children of Israel; and I will bless them."

(Numbers 6:27)

✳ *Cohen* (כהן) is Hebrew for "priest and literal descendant of Aaron"

Spiritual Vision
של הכהן גדול
Contents

Scriptural References
and
Their Abbreviations

Old Testament
Gen. - Genesis
Ex. - Exodus
Lev. - Leviticus
Num. - Numbers
Deut. - Deuteronomy
Josh. - Joshua
Judg. - Judges
1 Sam. - 1 Samuel
2 Sam. - 2 Samuel
1 Kgs. - 1 Kings
2 Kgs. - 2 Kings
1 Chron. - 1 Chronicles
2 Chron. - 2 Chronicles
Ezra - Ezra
Neh. - Nehemiah
Job - Job
Ps. - Psalms
Prov. - Proverbs
Eccl. - Ecclesiastes
Isa. - Isaiah
Jer. - Jeremiah
Ezek. - Ezekiel
Dan. - Daniel
Zeph. - Zephaniah
Zech. - Zechariah
Mal. - Malachi

New Testament
Matt. - Matthew
Mark - Mark
Luke - Luke
John - John
Acts - Acts
Rom. - Romans, Epistle to the
1 Cor. - 1 Corinthians

2 Cor. - 2 Corinthians
Gal. - Galatians
Eph. - Ephesians
Philip. - Philippians
Col. - Colossians
1 Thes. - 1 Thessalonians
2 Thes. - 2 Thessalonians
1 Tim. - 1 Timothy
Heb. - To The Hebrews
James - Epistle of James
1 Pet. - 1 Peter
2 Pet. - 2 Peter
1 Jn. - 1 John
Jude - Jude
Rev. - Revelation

Book of Mormon
1 Ne. - 1 Nephi
2 Ne. - 2 Nephi
Jacob - Jacob
Mosiah - Mosiah
Alma - Alma
3 Ne. - 3 Nephi
Morm. - Mormon
Ether - Ether
Moro. - Moroni

D&C-Doctrine and Covenants

Pearl of Great Price
Abr. - Abraham
Moses - Moses

JST-Joseph Smith Translation

Prolegomena

What could be more pertinent than an exploration of spiritual vision that culminates with a striking view of the Adamic language? Experience proves that there is nothing worse than the inability to see with one's spiritual eyes. This is why the first words spoken by the Lord in His Sermon on the Mount were, *"Blessed are the poor in spirit."* He knew that spiritual poverty was pitch black, and that the hopeless would likely turn to Him, the only source of everlasting hope. What inspired this work was an importunate desire to share some spiritual vision, only after the authors suffered and groveled without it, and then found what was not a dissight for sore eyes. The ultimate form of vision is hope, especially when there is zero evidence to support it (faith—Heb. 11:1). To have faith, one must understand and see things as they really are, not from the perspective of fears, fantasies, and false doctrines. This requires an open and honest heart, correct thinking, experience, hard work, and divine influence.

and only the spirit knows how things really are

One author was born and raised in The Church of Jesus Christ of Latter-day Saints. He valiantly fulfilled a full-time mission to Japan, but was not truly converted until age 35. What tripped him up was personal tragedy (loss of loved ones) concurring with a peaked awareness by age 30 that contradictions existed in the scriptures. Factors that fueled this crescendo of consciousness concerning contradiction included:

- An upbringing by the "Mormon Rabbi"
- Serving in the Orient where millions of people did not know who Jesus Christ was let alone Joseph Smith
- Firsthand exposure through his professional training to a wide spectrum of medical anomalies that do not "fit the system," his own sister suffered from one of them
- A friend and medical school classmate who committed suicide over the Adam–God theory
- Apostate spouse, in-laws, and friend
- Assiduous study of the scriptures and Church history

What was most baffling was the contradiction that he observed within each entity. Much to his chagrin, others did not see the contradiction, or care to see it, or did not seem to understand why it was there, or could not explain it enough to satisfy him. It was not until 1997 that he finally had a breakthrough only after treading his own winepress.

Joseph Smith translated in 2 Nephi 2:11, *"For it must needs be that there is an opposition in all things,"* but when he explained it, there was no mention of internal opposition. For example, there is a God so there must also be a devil, but if there is opposition in **all** things, then would not there be opposition in God, Himself? When it says, *"in all things,"* does it mean in the scriptures and prophets too? In the same chapter it states that Satan is the father of all lies, but it does not say he is the father of all contradiction. What is the difference between a lie, a contradiction, and opposition, if any? Could the lie be that the Church is not true because of contradiction? All of this raced through the author's mind, but nothing he heard or read could explain it.

Paul confirmed that there is opposition from within. In Romans chapter 7, he gives the gospel equivalent of Newton's third law: *"For the good that I would, I do not: but the evil which I would not, that I do....I find then a **law**, that, when I would do good, evil is present with me....Oh wretched man that I am!"* Yet he never explains how or why. Even the Lord felt the pull in the opposite direction when He did good (Luke 6:19; 8:46; 22:42–44; Matt. 26:38–39). Nephi also expressed his wretchedness and that his heart sorrowed because of his flesh (2 Nephi 4:17). Is the flesh in opposition with the spirit via the fall for probationary purpose?

When the author had his patriarchal blessing at age 18, he already was vexed with this issue of contradiction, but he suppressed it. If there is any shred of doubt that patriarchs are inspired, this is what he was told in his blessing: *"The Lord knows the perplexing and disturbing problem prevalent in your mind and heart at this time, and so I bless you that all will be well so far as your mission in life is concerned....The Lord blesses you with an abundance of strength so strong that in all the experiences of life, no power or influence will be able to impede your work,..."*

Part one of this book expresses the denouement of the author's spiritual quandary. It commences with a rather visceral discussion on feelings, which are the vital signs of the heart, and then gives a plethora of examples of apparent contradiction in the scriptures, which play their role in producing "mists of darkness" here in mortality. It continues with an elaboration on faith and moral agency and their relationship to contradiction, and then finishes with explanations on the paradoxical issues that deserve further attention. Thus, part one is called "Contradiction and the Three F's: Feelings, Faith, and Freedom." Ideally, the reader should research the scriptural references given, in order to have a better comprehension of what the author is attempting to communicate.

The reader might also pay particular attention to the section immediately following the contradiction cornucopia. It is there that the crux of the divine breakthrough is expressed. This includes the complete correction of the mistranslation at the end of Hebrews chapter 11, which would be the greatest discourse on faith in the scriptures if it were not for the mistranslation. Hopefully, Paul is now pleased! As an insightful aside, the author confesses that some time prior to his enlightenment, he threw his scriptures across the room out of utter disgust and frustration over the way the end of the chapter read. This was even with Joseph Smith's translation, because he knew there was something critical still missing but was not sure he would ever find out.

Chapter four is certainly a far cry from being a complete exposition on the issues posed. It is merely the author's insights on some rather complex and abstruse questions. Consequently, there may be holes or cryptic reasoning that could lead to misunderstandings. It is not ours to have a complete vision in this life (1 Cor. 13:12), merely sufficient, in the same way we may be 20/20 in a three dimensional world but not see like an eagle, or better yet, in other dimensions. Because we must walk by faith, there are mysteries that will remain inscrutable. Peter's example reminds us that things do not have to make perfect sense. In John 6, Jesus proclaims, *"Whoso eateth my flesh, and drinketh my blood, hath eternal life,"* which offended the multitude, and even left the Twelve bewildered. Yet when Jesus asked them if they were going to leave as the multitude did, Peter replied, *"Lord, to whom shall we go?...Thou art that Christ, the Son of the living God."*

The overall purpose of part one is to establish a vital spiritual foundation, without which, the full import and validity of the truths presented in part two would go unappreciated. In fact, many of the truths expressed later on in the book would have remained undiscovered by the authors without an understanding of those in part one.

Joseph Smith and his teachings have been stacked up many times against Christendom as the captious world knows it, but what about Judaism? After the first author was truly converted, he became increasingly aware from personal study and doctrinal discussions with the "Mormon Rabbi," the other author, of parallels between Judaism and Mormonism that support the authenticity of Joseph Smith's ministry. A true prophet of God requires no proof, but when all is said and done, the evidence is there. Both authors agreed that these overlaps should be compiled and published. Hence, the second part of the book entitled, "Overlapping Judaism with Mormonism." This imbrication is particularly illuminating for the Jewish investigator seeking milk from the mormon coconut, and also provides a delicious piquant sauce for the Latter-day Saints who are hankering to dress up their steaks. Nevertheless, as the presentation used in part two is oriented more for the Latter-day Saints than the Jews, it may have to be restructured to be an ideal missionary tool for the Jews.

Part two starts with the nature of God, continues with the stick of Joseph and the Urim and Thummim, and then discusses Elias and Elijah and some Jewish traditions. It concludes however with an unprecedented outlook on the original Hebrew or the Adamic language. This revolutionary view includes the accurate pronunciation of the Lord's name, and also the link between genetics, the alphabet, and the Godhead. In order to apreciate the implications of this, one has to only consider that the Adamic language will be used in the millenium (Zeph. 3:9), and that without the original alphabet, we would not exist today (Hugh Nibley's *Temple and Cosmos*, p. 458).

The Mormon Rabbi's unique upbringing by a rabbi whose native tongue included Yiddish, along with his unremitting study of the scriptures after his conversion, were indispensable to the completion of part two. His conversion to the Church was a miracle in and of itself, and the sacrifices that he made to be a member are staggering, including loss of parents, sisters, wife, daughter, and employment. The truth is that since his conversion, he has dedicated his entire life to the Church and to missionary work, at the expense of all else, for better or for worse. He has touched the lives of literally thousands of people, many of them non-members who joined the Church largely because of his influence. There has not been a bolder, more fearless missionary in the Church, and this is because of his natural, God-given audacity (*chutzpah*).

This same intrepidity, when it was set aflame by an intuitive awareness that Judaism was a dead religion because it had not had a prophet for 2400 years, gave him the courage to abdicate from Judaism. While serving in Korea as a dentist during the Korean War, a fellow dentist named Junius Gibbons introduced him to the Church by first teaching him that the Jews represent only one tribe of Israel, and that Junius was not a Gentile, but a fellow Israelite. Junius then gave him a Book of Mormon and asked him to read it along with the 53rd chapter of Isaiah. After completing his homework, Irving applied the promise in Moroni 10:3–5, and sure enough, through divine revelation as promised, it was revealed to him that the Book of Mormon is true and that Jesus is the Messiah. He wept for days.

It is the sincere hope of the authors that this work will be instrumental in increasing the faith of the members and helping investigators, particularly those who are Jewish, over certain hurdles that may have been otherwise insurmountable. May it also quiet some critics, and even nudge them, as well as the silently dissentient towards a *rapprochement* with the Church. Since the two parts are on disparate, yet complementary subjects, the book should have broader influence.

For the restored gospel to have its greatest sway, and since God's house is a house of order, the mesh between the dispensation of the fullness of times and all previous dispensations must be perfected, and a recapitulation of past dispensations in this one is vital. Notwithstanding its limitations, the authors believe this work is another step in that direction, and they look forward to the rod coming forth out of the Stem of Jesse (Isa. 11:1; D&C 113).

We look through the eyes of visionaries including our Creator, and without them, this book would not have been possible. That being stated, the book does have some new and exciting illuminations and amplifications of certain doctrinal truths. This should come as no surprise and without deprecation, for we believe that there is more to be revealed and seek after anything praiseworthy or of good report. The beauty of truth is that it finds a way, speaks for itself, and is ageless, a refreshing contrast to ephemeral fads, fashions, and false doctrines, which pall with the passing of time.

Yet there is a downside to discovering truth: most advances are made on the fringes of uncertainty, and therefore, truth is shut out without human error (Morm. 9:31). Alas, there is still much to be learned, and some of the truths presented here may need further refinement.

Naturally, a goal of the authors from the inception of this work was to avoid fluff, repetition, and duplication, and thereby have a more concise, distilled, and original message. Thus, the book is smaller than it might have been, and the reading may be a bit heavy, or at times even intense, but this way the reader does not have to peruse several pages before finding what is probably wanted.

The title of the book does have sentimental value with both authors, one being an ophthalmologist who is moved by Paul's expression, "*If it had been possible, ye would have plucked out your own eyes and have given them to me*" (Gal. 4:14–15), Paul referring to his "*thorn in the flesh,*" but wishing to pluck out his spiritual eyes and give them to the Galatians (3:1). The other author believes that one of his ancestors, Eleazar, wrote the book of *Jasher,* which in the Hebrew means "illumination." Thus, *Jasher* is not the name of the author, and the English should read, *The Illuminated Book.* (The book of Jasher is mentioned in Josh. 10:13 when Joshua made the sun and the moon stand still by the power of the priesthood, and also in 2 Sam. 1:18.)

Although the authors are neither Hebraists nor linguists, they use both Hebrew and linguistics to reveal certain doctrinal pearls. Some mysteries are unlocked by solving Hebraic cryptograms. A cryptogram is a cloaked message written in code. For the readers who are novices at Hebrew, bear in mind that Hebrew is read from right to left. The authors prefer the Ashkenazi pronunciation—for example, the *tau* (t) is sometimes pronounced as an *s*—because at times it seems to be more reverent than the Sephardi.

Moreover, it is vital for the reader to understand that because of the scattering of Israel, there were many Hebraic sound shifts in the European languages, especially the Germanic which includes English. They consist of: *b* to *p* and *v*, *d* to *t* and *th*, *g* to *k* and *gh*, *p* to *f* and *pf*, *k* to *h* and *ch*, *t* to *th*, *ts*, *tz*, and *s*, *th* to *d*, and *s*, *sk*, and *st* to *sh* (Dr. Terry Blodgett, SUU). It is also crucial to remember that the English alphabet originated from the Hebrew, through Greek and Latin: the Hebrew alphabet starts with aleph, beth, gimel, daleth, and is listed below for reference. The reason for including the ו (o) and the ו (u) is given in chapter 11 after the stage has been set, even for Hebraists, with the preceding ten chapters.

Lastly, the authors would be remiss if they did not express gratitude here to the four general authorities who have had the most influence on their lives, for their inspiration and encouragement to search ever deeper for unique insights into the restored gospel: Elders Harold B. Lee, Neal A. Maxwell, Hartman Rector, Jr., and Marion D. Hanks. The authors also thank Arthur Arvanitas for his assistance on the Greek.

Hebrew Alphabet

א	- Aleph	ט	- Teth	פף	- Pe
ב	- Beth	י	- Yod	צץ	- Tzade
ג	- Gimel	כך	- Caph	ק	- Koph
ד	- Daleth	ל	- Lamed	ר	- Resh
ה	- He	מם	- Mem	ש	- Shin, Sin
ו	- Vav	נן	- Nun	ת	- Tau
ז	- Zain	ס	- Samech	(ו)	- o
ח	- Cheth	ע	- Ain	(ו)	- u

CONTRADICTION
AND
FEELINGS
FAITH
AND
FREEDOM

Chapter 1

Feelings

There are two types of blindness; victims of either cannot see the trees, let alone the forest, but the darker and more ominous form is spiritual. The aphorism *"Without vision, the people perish"* (Prov. 29:18) pertains to this blindness of the heart. The salient features are an absence of faith, hope, love, peace, proper perspective or purpose, where people are **past feeling** of righteous, godlike desires (Eph. 4:18–19; 1 Ne. 17:45; Moro. 9:20), have no stabs of conscience, and every imagination of their petrified hearts is only evil (Gen. 6:5). The culminating sign is the thirst for blood (Gen. 4:8; 37:18; John 8:40; 1 Ne. 17:44; Moro. 9:5; D&C 135:4). Alas, spiritual blindness augurs badly, for the blind cannot be roused from their spiritual hebetude, and retribution rarely fails in the pursuit of evil. Thus

Lucifer has those who are blinded "checkmated," or at least in a "zugzwang" crying craven.

In contrast, the partially sighted are insinuated between two mighty opposites, and being rent with conflict, they experience a farrago of emotions including: restlessness, doubt, confusion, bewilderment, vacillation, indecision, and ennui. They "stare at their navels" and can see the trees, but not the forest. They are not bereft of feelings while traversing *mists of darkness,* but have a mix, and **feel** their way either to the great and spacious building or to the tree of life via the iron rod (1 Ne. 8:24, 31).

Those who see dimly with their hearts are only partly engaged, not absolutely plighted, and find themselves seduced by *"wells without water"* (diversions/false gods with no relish of salvation), and turn like dogs to their own vomit (2 Pet. 2:17, 22). Moreover, they mistrust divinely given apprehensions, and fail to doff their rose-colored glasses from noses retroussé. Thus, they blithely underestimate the war against the soul or their vulnerability, and the power of the dark side (1 Pet. 5:8; 2 Ne. 28:7–8, 21–24). As Byron Fowles so beautifully expressed, *"Behold the host delighting to deprave, who track the steps of glory to the grave."* Alas, the partially sighted fall into "check," or even a "spiritual stalemate" by the Adversary, and surprised, they glance at him askance. Lastly, those without "perfect vision" can have a testimony, yet not be finished with the segue to true conversion, Peter being a prime example (John 6:67–69; 18:25–27).

This illustrates the crucial role of feelings here in mortality, even after we partake of the fruit. (1 Ne. 8:28; Rom. 1:16; 5:5; Philip. 1:20; D&C 6:23; 9:8–9). There is a difference between shame and guilt, and it is not just a matter of semantics. Guilt is a feeling of remorse after recognizing a wrongdoing. Shame can be felt without making a mistake. The world considers all shame pathological, but Jeremiah felt his days were consumed with shame (20:18), and saints who endured the crosses of the world (2 Ne. 9:18) and even the Lord (Heb. 12:2) despised the shame of it. Shame is a complex emotion, not always bad according to the scriptures.

Yet there is a false side to shame. Some who partook of the fruit of the tree of life in Lehi's dream felt shame after being scoffed at. Paul analyzed it for himself and was convinced that through hope he was not ashamed of the gospel of Jesus Christ. There are other precursors of pernicious shame besides a deficiency of hope:

1. A smidgen of envy for the sinner: residual love for the things of the world (Matt.13:22)
2. Discomfiture with opposition (1 Cor. 4:14; Matt. 13:21), especially within ourselves: not completely accepting its inevitability or understanding why it is there
3. Hypersensitivity to one's own weaknesses: not understanding that God's strength is made perfect in weakness, the consummate example being that Christ *"was crucified through weakness,"* but resurrected by the

power of God (2 Cor. 12:9; 13:4)
4. Feeling like a burlesque of previous hopes and dreams: attachment to outcomes in this life
5. Skeletons in the closet that haunt a person: even if God remembers them no more, Lucifer never forgets and would use them to arrogate dominion over us (Rev. 12:10)

Thus there is godly shame and destructive shame, just as there is godly sorrow and the sorrow of the damned (2 Cor. 7:10; Morm. 2:13). Anger is another emotion that works both ways; usually it is ugly, but not always (Ex. 32:19; Num. 25:4; Mark 3:5; 1 Ne. 17:35; 22:16). Not only may one emotional type work good or evil, righteous feelings can be mixed—such as feelings about war and the price of freedom, or the delicate balance between justice and mercy.

Feelings and emotions are a function of the spirit, and the vital signs of the heart. They take precedence over the physical senses or the intellect, because they not only reveal who we really are, but help us see *"things as they really are"* (Jacob 4:13), and ultimately, it is feelings more than intellect or sensations that determine opinion. Hence, the Lord teaches: *"Blessed are the pure in heart,"* as well as *"Their hearts are far from me"*; *"Judge not with your eyes or your ears, but with your heart"*; and *"Open your hearts that ye may understand."* Moreover, by having to rely on feelings, we are on stage without a script, our moral agency is preserved, and we learn to walk by faith.

Yet the heart, mind, and body are linked (Philip. 2:2; D&C 9:7–9), and our thoughts and sensations affect our feelings. This is why splintering forces such as scholarly and career pursuits can undermine our faith, and sensuality and substance abuse can "feel good," yet leave us spiritually bankrupt. Contradistinctively, scripture study, prayer, and fasting foster spirituality, which is light and truth (D&C 84:45) and a testimony of Jesus Christ (Rev. 19:10).

The scriptures are not only filled with spiritual opiates, but their study results in mental lustration. Poor understanding will impede our spiritual growth, and "stinking thinking" is bad vision, which is looking at things from the perspective of fears, fantasies, and false doctrines. Not only is correct thinking indispensable, but also an ever deeper and broader understanding, for the sciolist, who has only a smattering of knowledge, is handicapped by small-mindedness.

We can learn much from the citizens of the City of Enoch who were not only of one heart, but also of one mind (Moses 7:18). Ultimately the mind and the heart have to perfectly mesh, and our goal is to have correct thoughts that match righteous feelings, which results in righteous acts. Incorrect thoughts that contradict righteous feelings and correct thoughts that contradict evil feelings are the easiest to identify because they cause the most symptoms. Take the expressions: *I know what I ought to do but I don't want to do it; my heart says yes but my head says no;* or, *fake it till you make it.* On the other hand, "stinking thinking" and evil feelings are mutual lovers, and therefore more insidious—for example, prejudice and pride; pessimism and hopelessness; or, intellectualism and Pyrrhonism. Finally, even if the mind and spirit are willing, there is always the flesh to contend with (Matt. 26:41).

The fast, which includes prayer, is a potent stimulus of spirituality because it knocks the natural man to his knees. This is because there are only two physical drives stronger than hunger and thirst, and they are the desire to respire and temperature regulation. All other physical appetites, including the sex drive, ultimately bow to hunger and thirst. Most fasts are for 24 hours or less, and during that time period, glucose, an essential nutrient for the brain, is derived from the glycogen stores in the liver. Fasts for longer durations result in catabolism of body proteins to sythesize glucose (gluconeogenesis), and catabolism of body lipids, which causes ketosis. There have been only three people known to have survived a fast of 40 days and 40 nights. They are Moses (twice), Elijah, and Jesus. The only way they survived that length of a fast is by transfiguration (Ex. 34:30–35), and/or partaking of heavenly alchemy/sacrament prior to fasting (Ex. 24:11; 1 Kgs. 19:5–8).

Other pearls about spirituality are that it must be exercised and nourished or else it falls into atrophy and desuetude, and although it can be discovered and nurtured in solitude, it can only blossom and be fulfilled in community. Not only can spiritual assets be triturated, there are certain hurdles in life over which we all need help, and we strengthen and edify each other, because we all have different gifts (1 Cor. 12; Luke 22:32).

Another characteristic of the City of Enoch was that there were no poor among them. This is not only because the rich shared, but also everyone was industrious: nobody was enervated by sloth and nimiety. The fainéant and otiose became extinct, as well as arrivistes, parvenus, and even sinecures: there were no spirits lazier than their bodies. The importance of hustle and hard work for spirituality cannot be exaggerated. Consequently, the future of any society is in its middle class.

In the pursuit of spirituality, the value of experience cannot be overestimated. When Adam and Eve partook of the fruit of the tree of knowledge of good and evil, Elohim had Jehovah place cherubim and flaming sword to guard the tree of life lest Adam and Eve partake of its fruit and live forever in their sins. Joseph Smith revealed that the fruit of the tree of life is the Atonement, and the tree of life represents the love of God (1 Ne. 11:22–25), or His Only Begotten Son (John 3:16). Alma instructed that Adam and Eve needed to be prepared by passing through sorrow before they could benefit from the Atonement (Alma 12:26). Paul taught: *"Tribulation worketh patience, and patience, experience, and experience, hope: And hope maketh not ashamed; because the love of God* [tree of life] *is shed abroad in our hearts by the Holy Ghost which is given unto us"*(Rom. 5:3–5). In other words, we would neither know the good from the evil, nor appreciate the Atonement without experience with adversity, and so we would indeed, live forever in our sins without the excursion through *the lone and dreary world.* In order for the Atonement to have effect, we must admit our nothingness without it, and that we are weak and unprofitable, and then turn to God to fill the void. This opens up a new world for us, for not only does the Atonement begin to take effect, but also our weaknesses start yielding to strength (2 Cor. 12:9; Ether 12:27). Joseph Smith taught: *"For what doth it profit a man if a gift is bestowed upon him, and he receive not the gift? Behold, he rejoices not in that which is given unto him, neither rejoices in him who is the giver of the gift"* (D&C 88:33).

There are two other things that rob us of the Atonement other than the lack of experience enduring affliction: not repenting (D&C 19:15–20), and not forgiving (Matt. 7:1–2; D&C 64:9–10). Pettifoggers, who rob others of the Atonement by encouraging them not to forgive, are children of Lucifer himself.

Once we appreciate the Atonement and then repent, and forgive, there are two things that give us "extra credit" concerning it: missionary work (D&C 4:4; 15:6; 18:15) and charity (1 Pet. 4:8).

Finally, to follow are some statistics from Global Renaissance Alliance just to demonstrate how perspective affects our feelings. Keep in mind as you read them that the feeling and attitude of gratitude could and should ultimately exist independent of how others are faring around us, and that the first requirement to be numbered with God's people is the desire to bear one another's burdens, mourn with those who mourn, and comfort those who stand in need of comfort (Mosiah 18:8–9).

*Only one percent of the world has a computer and the equivalent of a college education. If you have never experienced the danger of battle, the loneliness of imprisonment, the agony of torture, or the pangs of starvation, you are ahead of 500 million people in the world. If you can attend a church meeting without fear of harassment, arrest, torture, or death, you are more blessed than three billion people in the world. If you have food in the refrigerator, clothes on your back, a roof overhead, and a place to sleep, you are richer than 75 percent of the world. If you have money in the bank, in your wallet, and spare change in a dish someplace, you are among the top ten percent of the world's wealthy.

In summation, since we move by "feel" in this life, it is expedient that we connect the mind to the heart, *hence* and become more skilled with our "sixth sense" and *the guidance* conscious of our feelings, even the suppressed subliminal ones. If so, we may not only have a better understanding of how the Lord works, but also where we *of the* stand in relation to Him. Hopefully, we will then do *Holy* what we can to transform our feelings to resemble *Ghost* those of the Savior, and prepare our calloused hearts unto Him (1 Sam. 7:3).

Indeed, a spiritual renaissance sometimes concurs with and even requires a subjugation of certain emotions (such as fear and pride) that encumber us, and crimp our progress or hold us hostage under spiritual duress. Circumcision of the heart (2 Ne. 9:33) and the metamorphosis of feelings are not an easy process given their visceral nature. They usually require prayer and fasting in the short run, decades of righteous living in the long run, and the "blessing" of adversity (dung in Jacob 5:47, 64 and Philip. 3:8; fatigue in Alma 17:5).

As the feelings and desires of our hearts more closely mirror those of the Savior, we will taste more of the *fruit of the spirit* (Gal. 5:22), the eyes of our understanding will be enlightened, and we will be able to see the forest through the trees, and over and around those mists of darkness. It is then that we will be truly converted and the natural man crucified (Gal. 5:24). Emerged from our spiritual chrysalises, our love for others flowers, and our spiritual magnetism draws them in our wake.

One last consideration is the colors of feelings, which are only appreciated with our spiritual cones. By the end of chapter three, it will be apparent that faith is blood red and hope is purple, while fear is black, and doubt is pale gray. Patience, meekness, longanimity, and equanimity all have blue hues. When we feel alive and energized, or nourished and content, we emit a verdurous wavelength: gratitude is green. Love evolves from coquette to a coral blush, then to saffron, and finally to crimson. Peace, integrity, and charity (1 Cor. 13) are a scintillating white. Notice that the *fruit of the spirit* (Gal. 5:22) has all of the colors of the rainbow (Rev. 4:2–3), and together emits bright glowing **light** that casts no shadow (James 1:17; Alma 7:20), but evil feelings are different shades of gray, including black. Even if spiritual light cannot be seen with our physical eyes, it can be felt with our hearts.

Chapter 2

Contradiction and Moral Agency

If navigating through *mists of darkness* (2 Pet. 2:17) is indeed so parlous a journey that even the elect are deceived (Matt. 24:24), then it is expedient that we understand them better. To deceive even the elect, Satan speaks almost the truth, twists it, or puts a spin on it, and makes *"winding approaches to temptation and slippery paths to depravity"* (J. Mackintosh). The following is a spiritual callisthenic consisting of a series of questions in order to illustrate just how disenchanting and stupefying these miasmas are here in mortality. The exercise will also increase their palpability and show how easy it is to twist or shade the truth. It is not critical that one relates to all of the examples in this exercise, only some, and it is important to keep in mind that these examples are not exhaustive. Many of them loom large in the mind of any thinking person, and have been or will be voiced by investigators, dissenters, and even our children or significant other.

Why was it right for Nephi to kill Laban, Phinehas to kill Zimri and Cozbi (Num. 25), or Teancum to kill the nefarious Amalikiah (Alma 51), but God severely punishes the facinorous Cain for murdering Abel? Or why would God ask Abraham to sacrifice Isaac if murder is so evil?

Abraham told Abimelech a white lie that Sarah was his sister, and Rebekah and Jacob deceived Isaac about the birthright (Gen. 27), and it was counted for righteousness, but deception is wrong and God cannot lie (Heb. 6:18). Rahab lied about the spies' whereabouts in Jericho (Josh. 2:4–6), and David lied to Achish that he had attacked the Israelites (1 Sam 27:10–12), and Rahab and David were blessed for it, but lying is wrong and God cannot lie (Ether 3:12).

Christ taught us to turn the other cheek and love our enemies, yet it was right to wipe out an entire nation including women, children and animals (1 Sam. 15). How could both the Nephites and the Anti-Nephi-Lehis have a righteous response to Lamanite aggression? It is right to take up arms and defend our country, yet *"war hath no fury like a non-combatant"* (Charles Edward Montague). Christ taught that he who lives by the sword must die by the sword, yet *"one sword keeps another in its sheath"* (George Herbert). Why is peace sometimes worth fighting for? Why was war allowed in heaven (Rev. 12:7)? Why is religion a cause of so much bloodshed?

Why would Joseph Smith, a prophet of God, translate a sermon denouncing polygamy in the book of Jacob, yet later champion it with the "New and Everlasting Covenant" and 40+ wives? Furthermore, why would he, much to Emma's consternation, not tell her about some of them and blame it on "spiritual wifery" (B. Carmon Hardy's *Solemn Covenant: The Mormon Polygamous Passage*), or not let her suggest it, or even consent to it, as it was with Abraham and

Jacob? Or why would he compare himself to Moses even though Moses ended up with only one wife (Zipporah) under the covenant? Finally, why would he ask for Heber Kimball's wife, but adultery is such a grievous sin?

Why would the Mormon Church spend tithing money on the construction of great and spacious buildings when there are people dying of starvation in the world? Coffee is against church standards, but obesity is not, even though it is a greater health hazard. Why would the Church publish the "Proclamation on the Family" when there are people in this world who cannot have a family or who are not sure of their gender because of some medical anomaly? If the Church were true then why did Church officials not know Hoffman was a fraud? If the Church were true, then why in Utah has the suicide rate among young men, the closet homosexuality rate among men, the pregnancy rate among unmarried young women, and the children in single parent homes been one of the highest per capita in the nation?

Why would Jesus raise Lazarus from the dead and not John the Baptist, a cousin and closer friend than Lazarus? Abraham was saved from death but Abinadi was not, even though both wanted and deserved to be saved. The Lord spared Alma and Amulek, but not the other righteous in Ammonihah. Why would the Lord feed manna to the children of Israel and not save the Martin Handcart Company? Is AIDS a plague even though innocent children and hemophiliacs are stricken?

How about the concept that all men are created equal but some are more equal than others? Or God loves us all the same but he aggrandizes a chosen people? Which is worse, to have it all, lose it all, and then gain it all back (Job), or to never have (Elephant Man)? If God judges with His heart and not His eyes, why did He reward Job's righteousness with the fairest daughters in the land (Job 42:15)?

Is God the male chauvinist or is man the perpetrator of masculine preeminence and prerogative? Why can chivalry be the most delicate form of contempt? Why does raising the voice lower the level of conversation (Stanley Horowitz)? Why are love and hate so intimately connected? Because of the machinations and perturbations of love, a murder is most likely to be committed by a once-loving spouse. The oxymoron "cruel kindness" has validity. God is love but He hates the wicked (1 John 4:8; Heb 1:9). Your best friend has the potential to become your worst enemy.

What is the real difference between insanity and wickedness? Is a vision a revelation or a hallucination? Why is religion such a heady wine? Why is it righteous for some people to take drugs, but evil for others? Christ stressed humility, yet He left no question as to His divinity. What about the fine line between being meek and pucilanimous? Is a windfall a blessing or luck? How are God's paths straight, yet His course is one eternal round (Alma 37:12; D&C 3:2)? Why would Jesus call Judas to be an apostle if He knew Judas would betray Him? If there are three degrees of glory, then where does God draw the line so that nobody just misses an A or a B? If now is the time for man to prepare to meet God (Alma 34:32–34), then why would 99.9 percent of God's children be allowed to go through life without the gospel?

Why are happiness and sorrow not mutually exclusive in this life? How come sometimes when you win you lose and sometimes when you lose you win? Or why has success made failures out of many (Cindy Adams)? And why is a measure of success how high you bounce after hitting bottom (George Smith Patten)? Moreover, how is it that when you are weak, then you are strong (2 Cor. 12:10)? Why are problems the seeds of opportunity? Why is there no courage without fear (Mark Twain)? Or why is the greatest risk taking no risk at all? Finally, in the long run, why does ugliness pall almost as much as beauty (George Saintsbury)?

Why would Brigham Young stress the validity of the Adam–God theory in his discourses, but Joseph Fielding Smith adamantly denounce the theory in his *Doctrines of Salvation*? Why would Joseph Smith preach in his "King Follett Discourse" that intelligence, which can neither be created nor destroyed, is equivalent to the mind, even though there are such conditions as strokes and Alzheimer's disease?

How about the contrast between going through more than one marriage yet never engaging in premarital sex, and only being intimate with one person both inside and outside marriage? Why is adultery evil, but marrying another person after your spouse dies is not?

How about the concept that you can be happily married to more than one unique individual who exists on this earth even if it is only a handful, but God expects you to be committed to only the one person you are married to and you could only have the children that you have with that person? And what if your spouse perished in the war in heaven or on earth? If it is not good for man to be alone, then why would Paul teach, *"Art thou loosed from a wife? seek not a wife"* (1 Cor. 7:27), and why would Jeremiah be commanded not to take a wife (Jer. 16:2)?

There is one thing all of these have in common: they are examples of contradiction, inconsistency, incongruity, inconsonance, paradox, dichotomy, opposition, irony, uncertainty, or whatever else you want to call it, including the vogue locution, "situational ethics." A paradox is a seemingly contradictory proposition, but in reality, an expression of truth. Contradiction is truth inside out, camouflaged or masked to most, yet in neon lights to a select few. It is like a stereogram with a real picture inside of a nonsense image. It is truth standing on its head to get attention. The reality is that there are apparent contradictions all throughout the scriptures and ever since God's dealings with man, and this is the primary reason why the world thinks the scriptures are mythopoeic and wonders if religious bouffe could go to greater lengths. What is the Lord concealing from some and yet simultaneously inculcating into the hearts of others? What truth has He cloaked for some greater purpose? How does Satan use that to deceive us?

The truth is that God is inconsistently consistent in the way he deals with man and he has created a perfectly imperfect world. Why? **Contradiction perfects our moral agency and our faith.** It allows us to rationalize any behavior and thus the dissolute aspects of human nature and the effluvia and moral turpitude of a sick society spew forth. It is no wonder we live in a world that spawns forth terrorists, commits holocausts, and crucifies our Lord. This is perfect moral agency, even if God does have an acute prescience for how we will act. It is the genius of the whole plan, the heart of the plan being the Atonement, and the Lord was bound to provide it, for where the Spirit of the Lord is there is liberty (2 Cor. 3:17). There can be found just as many reasons to believe as there are not to believe. If everything made perfect sense to man, if there were no contradiction, inconsistency, paradox, irony, dichotomy, opposition, or incongruity, then we would be compelled to be righteous. We would have neither freedom nor faith; they are inseparably linked. This was Satan's plan: good things would only happen to good people and bad things would only happen to bad, and everything would be black and white. We would be compelled to do the right thing and we would need no faith. We would not be on stage without a script and therefore, we would not show our true colors and desires. Why does the Lord repeatedly say, *"Oh ye of little faith!"* He knew that because there is an element of perfect sovereignty here in mortality regardless of our genes or our circumstances (Neal A. Maxwell), we had to have perfect faith to endure to the end.

What about the contradictions that arise from human error? They also fit into God's plan of freedom/faith perfection. In fact, God has set up the system here in mortality so that truth is shut out without human error (Morm. 9:31). The understanding of this is essential as we canvass the lives and teachings of prophets and priesthood leaders. Most advances are made on the threshold and in the twilight of uncertainty.

Our ultimate freedom springs from the contradiction and opposition inherent in each of us (Rom. 7; 2 Ne. 4). Because of the fall, the flesh is put in opposition to the spirit for probationary purposes (Rom. 5:12; 7:18,23–25; Matt. 26:41; 2 Ne. 4:17; Alma 12:31), and yet the fight is not against the flesh, but Lucifer and spiritual wickedness in high places (Eph. 6:12; 2 Ne. 4:27). Lucifer just uses the flesh to get to us. The opposition from within is the source of pure choice, and therefore, we should not fear it or be too troubled by it. Yet it must be respected, because it makes us vulnerable to temptation and our humanness inescapable here in mortality. It explains why there must be a falling away first, both individually and collectively (2 Thes. 2:3), why we all have felt the urge and yielded to sin, and why it is so difficult to judge without hypocrisy (John 8:7; Matt 7:1–2). It also means that shadow-boxing or sciamachy is inevitable. No wonder both Paul and Nephi exclaim, *"Oh wretched soul that I am!"* How many times must one slay the natural man?

Even God is not immune from internal conflict: *"And it repented the Lord that he had made man on the earth, and it grieved him at his heart"* (Gen. 6:6).

Chapter 3
Perfect Faith and Hebrews 11

mine in families + people

Perfect faith exists when there is zero evidence to support what you hope for and contradiction satisfies that requirement. Thus faith perfection is inherent in the system, which is ideal considering true conversion requires such faith. Yet what all this really boils down to is that because of contradiction, we only cross the goal line when we are detached from outcomes in this life, which is a short run by God's standards. Only this is a total, fiducial surrender to the Lord. Could it be that Moses saw the burning bush and Joseph was elevated from prisoner to prime minister of Egypt only after this surrender and detachment from outcomes?

Hebrews chapter 11 would be the greatest discourse on faith in the scriptures if it were not for mistranslations. Paul starts out giving examples of faith that were rewarded in this life, such as Joseph and Moses, but hits a grand slam at the end of the chapter when he illustrates ostensible contradiction by including **examples of faith that went unanswered.** In verse 35, for his first example, it states, *"and others were tortured, not accepting deliverance; that they might obtain a better resurrection."* The most common way of not accepting deliverance was to remain a Christian when given the choice between "Christianity and death" or "abdication and life." Paul completes the examples of faith that were not rewarded in this life, and then the mistranslations start flying in verses 39 and 40. Verse 39 states, *"And these all, **having obtained a good report through faith,** received not the promise:"* It should read, "And these all, obtained a good report through faith, **not accepting deliverance,**" to match verse 35.

The proof that *"received not the promise"* is a mistranslation, is that in Hebrews 6:12, Paul states, *"That ye be not slothful, but followers of **them who through faith and patience inherit the promises."*** In all of Paul's writings, wherever he uses the word promise(s), he usually is referring to the promise of, or promises associated with celestial glory in the next life, and occasionally to the Comforter in this life.   A stark example is Galatians chapter three, which states that the faithful, including the Gentiles, are the children of Abraham, and therefore inherit the promises made to Abraham—namely, of the Spirit in this life and union with Christ in the next. In other words, "the promises" refers to spiritual blessings that are reserved for the faithful, and since it is a **promise from God, the faithful ALWAYS inherit and ultimately receive** those blessings, which include, but are not limited to: a celestial body (D&C 76:70; 1 Cor. 15:39–42), a Urim and Thummim (D&C 130:9–11), and a mansion in the New Jerusalem with God, where there is no darkness and no sorrow, and God's love, joy, and admiration are forever existent (Rev. 21 and 22). A celestial body is neither destructible, nor in opposition with the spirit, and has incredible capabilities: it can fly at awesome speeds, see in more than three dimensions, hear sub-liminal sounds, read minds, think multiple thoughts simultaneously, and it continuously emits bright, glowing light that casts no shadow, just to mention a few celestial capacities. A Urim and Thummim allows one to know and understand all the mysteries of God, if one asks in faith with an honest heart (see chapter 8).

To continue with the above explanation, Hebrews 11:35 states that they did not accept deliverance in order to obtain a better resurrection. How could they hope for a better resurrection if they were not members of the true church, the only people who have a vision of celestial glory? Also, Hebrews 11:39 tells us that these saints were faithful. In Romans 10:14–17, Paul teaches that one cannot have faith unless he or she has heard the gospel, and Alma instructs in chapter 32 that if some have faith after hearing the good word, they will nourish their faith with discipleship unto everlast-ing life. Therefore, **the faithful represent those who have heard the gospel of Jesus Christ, accepted and embraced it, joined the true church, and remained steadfast,** so verse 39 is a glaring mistranslation. Had they not been members of the Kingdom, Paul would have said, "They **would have** died in faith," (had they been exposed to the gospel).

But in the last verse there is another glaring mis-translation worse than the previous one that vitiates the message of the sermon. It states, *"God having provid-ed some better thing for us, that they without us should not be made perfect."* What do these saints need us for? They demonstrated perfect faith: they believed

Handwritten margin note: They need the ordinance work in the temple done. (rotated)

and hoped without any evidence to support it all the way to the bitter end—death. A modern day example would be the Martin Handcart Company. A Book of Mormon example would be the saints in Ammonihah. And there are others. It should read, **"that we without them,"** with the "we" and "them" flip-flopped. **Their example perfects our faith because now we know we have to be detached from outcomes in this life. We need them to perfect our faith because we may not have to spill our blood, God having provided some better thing for us, but we must be ready in our hearts to die for the Messiah if need be.** (Notice that the terrorists try to imitate such passion in the name of Allah, but their intent is to destroy life, while ours is to preserve it.)

The notion that they needed us for their ordinance work, particularly baptism, is a specious one. Who are we to believe that these saints, similar to Paul (1 Cor. 4:11–13; 2 Cor. 11:24–27), who were already baptized and were tortured to death because of their faith, need us? We have yet to lose one drop of blood, and might never, fighting against sin. Neither had the congregation Paul was addressing. In the very next chapter, Paul finishes his exhortation by stating, *"Ye have not resisted unto blood, striving against sin"* **(12:4).** The only thing they need us for is to perfect our faith through their example.

The "they" in 11:40 not only represents members of the true church, but they were probably endowed Melchizedek priesthood holders as well, because Paul needed their examples to pump up the Melchizedek priesthood holders he was addressing. At least a half dozen times he refers to the recipients as *brethren* (2:12; 3:12; 10:19), and twice as *sons* (12:6–7). In fact, in 2:11 he refers to them as *sanctified brethren*, and in 3:1, *"holy brethren, partakers of the heavenly calling,"* Jesus being the High Priest of their profession. Moreover, in 6:10, Paul refers to them as *ministers to the saints*, and in 13:24 he asks them to give his regards to the saints.

Furthermore, Hebrews is the only "epistle" that Paul wrote that does not have an opening salutation with Paul identifying himself, because as Melchizedek priesthood holders, they all knew him, so no identification was needed. But Timothy knew him and Paul identified himself in his epistles to Timothy. Is it possible that Hebrews is a sermon that he gave to a general priesthood assembly? In 10:25 it states, *"Not forsaking the assembling of ourselves together, as the manner of some is; but **exhorting** one another."* He uses the word *exhorting* to mean preaching with the spoken word. In 13:22 it states, *"And I beseech you, brethren, suffer the word of **exhortation**: for I have written a letter unto you in few words."* Hebrews is not the letter, but a recording of Paul's speech; or if it is the letter, he used it to give the sermon.

There are actually even more indications that this probably was addressed to a Melchizedek priesthood assembly. It is the only writing that he authored that uses rhetorical phraseology including two poignant admonishments regarding the seriousness of falling away after receiving the higher priesthood (6:4–6;

10:26–31). It gives a distinct conception of the higher priesthood (5–7), referring to its oath in 7:21, and using the name *Melchizedek* more than any other book in the Bible. It discusses at length the Tabernacle ritual/temple endowment (8–10), making specific mention to the veil (6:19; 9:3; 10:20) and to the New and Everlasting Covenant (8:8, 13; 10:20; 12:24; 13:20).

Paul would only communicate this way if he were trying to pump up the Melchizedek priesthood holders. Many of them had just endured *"a great fight of afflictions"* (10:32), were made gazingstock by reproach (10:33), and took compassion for Paul's bonds, and took joyfully the spoiling of their goods (10:34). Their spirits were down and their faith was failing (10:35), but he assured them that if they remained steadfast, they would receive the promise of celestial glory (10:36; 9:15). Then in chapter 11 he gave the greatest discourse on faith in the scriptures, which included members like them who were not delivered, because he knew some of them might have a similar fate, as did Paul, Peter, and James, just to name a few. The persecutions were so severe back then, and the Dark Ages imminent, that it was imperative for Paul to deliver a masterpiece.

We must not erroneously conclude that Paul used "celestial bribery" on the saints. *Bribery* connotes doing the right thing for the wrong reason—reward. This Paul never preached, but rather he inculcated in their hearts to be righteous for righteousness sake—in other words, out of love of righteousness. This is apparent in all of his writings, including the book of Hebrews (Heb. 1:9). The Lord also taught that we should hunger and thirst after righteousness (Matt. 5:6).

Perhaps Paul entitled the exhortation, "To The Hebrews," because Melchizedek was the first Hebrew and therefore, all those who hold the Melchizedek priesthood are Hebrews because he is their spiritual progenitor. Thus it could have been entitled, "To All Melchizedek Priesthood Holders," but Paul called it "To the Hebrews" because it was obvious to the saints back then who the Hebrews were and it was more reverent to use the term *Hebrews*. If he had been writing to the Jews, it would state, "The Epistle to the Jews." When Paul refers to himself as *"an Hebrew of the Hebrews"* (Philip. 3:5), he means he is not only a Hebrew in the flesh, but also a Hebrew in spirit and belief.

There is one other salient and critical mistranslation in Hebrews chapter 11. In verse 13 it states, *"These all died in faith not having received the promises,"* but it should read, "These all died in faith not having received the promises **directly**" (like Abraham and Sarah did). They inherited the promises associated with celestial glory because they died in faith, and if they died in faith, they were members of the Kingdom. (See the third and fourth paragraphs of this chapter.) Moreover, verse 13 continues by saying, *"but having seen them afar off, and were persuaded of them, and embraced them, and confessed that they were strangers and pilgrims on the earth."* They embraced the gospel, were persuaded to live righteously, and were not of this world. So indeed, they did die in faith as members of the true church, and inherited the promises, for in verse 16, it says that they will be in the New Jerusalem in the celestial kingdom with God.

It is obvious that whoever translated the "epistle" to the Hebrews did not know who the Hebrews were, anything about the Melchizedek priesthood, the New and Everlasting Covenant, the endowment ordinance, or the New Jerusalem. Nor did they know that the promises refer to celestial glory, and that there was such a thing as a general priesthood assembly. But why should they? It is understandable why there were so many glaring mistranslations: the translators were doing the best they could to translate the writing in a way that made some sense to them, but it was an impossible task to get it correct without an understanding of the items above. In fact, because of the esoteric content, it was probably the most difficult book to translate in the New Testament, other than the book of Revelation, so we must not be too hard on the translators, just aware of their predicament.

Here is an example of a mistranslation in the book of Revelation, in order to illustrate just how challenging it can be to translate. In chapter 13, John gives information and clues about the beast, who is antichrist. Now that the computer age has arrived, it is obvious from verses 16 and 17 that the antichrist will compel people to buy or sell over the internet either via a microchip embedded in the hand or forehead, or with the token or code of the beast. John saw all this in a vision and wanted to warn the reader, so the simplest way to do it having never used the internet was to give the token or code of the beast, which in Hebrew is ווו. The Greeks came along and knew nothing about the worldwide web or the cryptogram for the beast, and so when they saw ווו they thought it symbolized 666, because ו is not only Hebrew for *W*, by the second century B.C. it was also Hebrew for the number *6* (Menahem Mansoor's *Biblical Hebrew,* vol. 1:15). But the Jews do not think of Hebrew names as having a numerical value, so there is no ostensible reason for John, a pure Jew, to think that the antichrist's name had a numerical value. Thus originally, verses 17 and 18 were not referring to the name or number of the beast but rather the token or code of the beast, which would be used in trading. The verses should read, "And no man might buy or sell, save he that had the mark, or the token or code of the beast. Here is wisdom. Let him that hath understanding know the code of the beast, for it is of man and is WWW." In summation, whoever **forces** people to use the worldwide web in order to buy or sell is the antichrist.

Accordingly, another place where the ווו probably showed up was on the Gold Plates in 3 Nephi 9:2, which Joseph Smith translated *"Wo Wo Wo."* It is highly significant that the Urim and Thummim spelled the word all throughout the Book of Mormon (the exception in 2 Ne. 1:13 is probably a transcription error) without an *e* when both the Oxford and Webster dictionaries only spell it with an *e*. There is more to the word *wo* than woe, and wherever it says "woe" in the

Bible (Matt. 23, etc.), it is probably a mistranslation and should read *wo*. (This is another evidence that Joseph Smith was a true prophet even if he did not know the full meaning—D&C 19:5 uses *woe*.) You see, Satan knew that ו (o) is a token of Jehovah who is *The Creator* (see pp. 135–136), and ו (u) is a token of the Holy Ghost (see pp. 73–74). Lucifer also wanted to get into the act, so he mutated the ו and the ו to ו, which he made his token; and to mimic the Godhead, he assigned his godhead, which comprises only him since he is a dictator, his token three times: ווו (*Wo Wo Wo*). Thus wherever it says *"Wo"* in the scriptures, it literally means the devil, and figuratively a cursing, and therefore it is usually followed by the word *unto*. This all rings true if one continues reading 3 Nephi 9:2 where the Lord says after all the destruction: *"Wo Wo Wo unto this people; wo unto the inhabitants of the whole earth except they shall repent: for the devil laugheth and his angels rejoice"* (compare Rev. 12:12). Therefore, *Wo*, or stronger yet, *Wo Wo Wo* is a proclamation by the Lord to the people of the world to repent and be righteous or else they will be in Satan's power. Comparatively Santa, a dyslexic form of Satan and an imposter of the Lord Jesus Christ, says *"Ho Ho Ho,"* but this means *"eat, drink, and be merry."*

Reverting to Hebrews, Joseph Smith only partially corrected the mistranslations at the end of Hebrews chapter 11 by adding that without their sufferings they could not be made perfect. But it continued to plague him, just as it did the author of this book. Joseph even used section 128 in the D&C to explain further his stance, but he admits in verse 18 that his explanation might have been **plainer.**

In D&C 128:15, he says that they need us for their ordinance work—specifically *baptism for the dead*—to be made perfect, and we need them with their ordinance work completed in order for us to be made perfect. He repeats in verse 18 of the same section that neither we without them nor they without us can be made perfect, and that the welding link is baptism for the dead. He was determined to convince the reader that the "they" in Hebrews 11:40 refers to those who died without the gospel, yet he sensed that those who died in the gospel had to fit in somewhere. He states: *"neither can they nor we be made perfect without those who have died in the gospel also,"* the "they," once again, referring to those who died without the gospel.

In summation, Joseph Smith eventually realized that the flip-flop of *they without us* in Hebrews 11:40 to *we without them* was important, but he never discovered the correct reason why, for he made the *faux pas* of thinking that the "they" referred to non-members needing baptism. This in no way detracts from his ministry as the leader of this dispensation. It only confirms that he was human, which actually makes his accomplishments even more impressive. Even in the front of the Book of Mormon, Joseph Smith translates, *"If there are faults, they are the mistakes of men."*

Faith stems the tedious tide of doubt, engenders righteous living, and unlocks priesthood power. That is why priesthood blessings are only for the faithful. Isn't it amazing that the Lord designed the Liahona to work by faith alone (1 Ne. 16:28–29; Mosiah 1:16; Alma 37:40)? What technology! Does faith emit a frequency of energy yet to be identified by man? Is there a Holy-ghost-ometer that works like a prism and measures our faith and spirituality by displaying the spectrum of spiritual light? If puny man can make a computer, imagine what God's computer is capable of.

hmm,

Faith is what propels us to endure no matter what the opposition. If we have faith, we cannot be conditioned to be any certain way, and the inverse is also true. Thus conditions do not make a man, they only shape him and reveal who he really is (William James). That is why B. F. Skinner, who expanded on Pavlov's work, has only part of the truth with his operant conditioning. He taught that a man could be conditioned to do anything; this is Satan's hope. If it were true, the prophets, who all have endured great hardships, would have given up their ministries. It is no wonder God's people are such a minority—the natural man takes the path of least resistance. What B. F. Skinner should have said is that the natural man can be conditioned to do anything—the spiritual man will resist one way or the other (Acts 9:5).

We must not think for a split second that it does not rend God's heart that so many of His spirit children go their own way, and then, consequently, their children and their children's children spend their whole lives without the gospel. But there is nothing that He can do because He is bound by the requirement of perfect moral agency in a probationary state. This is why missionary and temple work are valued so highly by the Lord.

Chapter 4

Understanding Some of the Mysteries

In order to understand the mysteries of God, one must have the Spirit of God (1 Cor. 2:11) and ultimately a Urim and Thummim (see chapter 8). Many of the questions posed previously are answered merely by understanding how God creates a world with an element of perfect liberty. But some of the questions deserve further explanation.

For example, we must understand why all men are created equal, but they are not. Egalitarianism only applies to our inalienable rights and the chance to be righteous and receive celestial glory, and one is only chosen because of righteousness. Conversely, the Lord expects more from the "chosen people." Righteousness is determined by what one does (numerator) with what one has been given (denominator). Thus, one can be exceedingly righteous, despite having exiguous resources, and limited capabilities or understanding (see stats on p. 27). Our activities in the pre-earth life largely determined our place of birth and family, but all this does not matter if one is not righteous. To be deemed righteous, more is expected from those with better circumstances. This is why it is difficult to know just how God is grading one's report card—because of the denominator (resources, capabilities, understanding, circumstances). As it approaches nothing, the total value of the person in God's eyes increases exponentially (Mark 12:43).

A case study fascinating by itself is Job, who had it all, then lost it all no fault of his own, only to gain it all back. He then was used as a prime example of patience and longanimity (James 5:11; D&C 121:10). Yet there are those who live their entire lives with virtually nothing no fault of their own (Elephant Man, slaves, etc.), or who have had and lost but never retrieved. It appears that for spiritual growth, having and losing is even more excavating than never having. Those who have always lacked are not sure what they are missing, so the cravings are less. Thus Shakespeare writes, *"It is better to have loved and lost, than to have never loved at all."* Moreover, recuperation and recovery seem to seal the faith-promotion of the trial, and may be dependent on detachment from outcomes in this life.

Most of us can understand how having or not having is largely but not completely contingent upon activities both in the pre-earth life and in mortality. But how does God determine who will have or not have independent of their activities in this life or the previous one? Many can comprehend that wherever a deficiency exists, there is an equal and opposite potential for growth. But how does God decide who gets what deficiencies? The Lord's declaration, "Ask and ye shall receive," was not "Ask and ye shall receive what you ask for when you ask for it." It only implies you will receive something that God wants you to have on His timetable. Yet in more ways than timing, God's gifts exceed expectations (Matt. 7:7–11; 3 Ne. 14:7–11).

One of the main reasons why the suicide rate among young men is so high in Utah (see p. 10), and why up to one out of 10 men in Salt Lake City lean toward alternative lifestyles, is related to attachment to outcomes while attempting to live the higher law that is not well understood. The pregnancy rate out-of-wedlock is also ironically high in Utah because of the combination of a higher standard, which does not require birth control, and complacency. The irony that these problems exist in a culture with a higher standard is really no different than the irony that murder is most likely to be committed by a spouse.

Another concept worthy of expression is the superimposition of foreordination on adventitious/aleatory events and blessings/cursings on luck (comes from the name *Lucifer*). God allows accidents to happen because it perfects our moral agency. An ideal example is a plane crash where 150 random lives are arbitrarily snuffed out of this world. But if someone is foreordained to do something and he has not yet had a chance to do it, either he will not be on that plane, or if he is, the plane will not crash, or he will miraculously survive the accident. Another example of chance events is an innocent victim of a plague as is the case with hemophiliacs and children with AIDS. Similarly, a throw of the dice seems to occur with our genes during reproduction producing nocuous mutations such as Down's syndrome and other *lusus naturae*. These events help perfect our moral agency and every time we witness a genetic or congenital anomaly we should thank that person and God in our hearts for the sacrifice being made for freedom/faith perfection (John 9:1–3).

The same sort of superimposure happens with relationships: some are foreordained of God, and the others occur from random encounters (Matt. 19:6; Luke 20:34). What makes the relationship collage even more mysterious is that there are some individuals who could be happy with anyone of a number of different people even though they could only have the children that they have with the person they are with (or the people they have been with), while there are those who could only be happy with one person in the whole world, and it is not always a matter of choice.

How honest can we really be? We turn a blind eye and pretend not to notice, and the exigencies of politeness and gentility can be at variance with candor and forthrightness. Moreover, those with selective memories are not sure if forgetfulness is a choice or an error, and society (even church) sometimes requires dissimulation of at least feelings and emotions for an increment of dignity. And how many times have we given credence to the gossip of an officious quidnunc, or admired a good storyteller who is merely an exaggerating fabulist. As Shakespeare said, *"If a lie may do thee grace, I'll gild it with the happiest terms I have,"* and *"Though it be honest, it is never too good to bring bad news."*

But Jeremiah observed: *"They will deceive everyone his neighbor, and will not speak the truth: they have taught their tongue to speak lies,"* and *"One speaketh peaceably to his neighbor with his mouth, but in heart, he layeth his wait"* (Jer. 9:5, 8). The truth is that the further our tongues drift away from our hearts, the closer we move towards Satan, and the difference between what we say and what we think and feel is a good inverse measure of not only our personal character, but also our society's moral fiber. It is not so much <u>a need to change our tongues to match our hearts as it</u> <u>is a change of heart to tame our tongues</u> (James 3:8). Oh, and let us ponder for a moment that the cruelest lies are sometimes told in silence, yet when God pleads the Fifth, He does so without lying (Ether 3:12; Heb. 6:18). Let's also not forget that God sees both the liminal and abstruse thoughts.

What about the sacred mendacity illustrated in the scriptures? Joseph, when he named Manasseh, (which means to forget), felt his selective memory regarding his family was a gift from God (Gen. 41:51). Abraham's white lie to Abimelech at his hostelry that Sarah was his sister was sacred (Gen. 20:2). Likewise, Jacob and Rebekah deceived Isaac regarding the birthright and it too was counted for righteousness (Gen. 27). Moreover, Rahab lied about the spies' whereabouts in Jericho (Josh. 2:4–6) and was blessed for it. David's mendacious response as to his activities in the land of Judah (1 Sam. 27:10–12) was essential to his survival, as well as his supporters'. Finally, Joseph Smith told the saints a half-truth that *Nauvoo* meant "City Beautiful" because he did not want to discourage them, but it actually means "we will come temporarily." Dare it be repeated, *moral agency preserved and perfected.*

Can we truly be good to all men when cruel kindness is a reality? Sometimes when life is busy and pressing, by helping one we may disregard another.

Juggling the needs of others and stewing from neglect are merely a part of the growth process here in mortality. What a great way to be stretched and excavated. It is even another element of freedom/faith perfection.

Let's probe deeper into this doctrine of three degrees of glory (1 Cor. 15:40). It is more than coincidence that there were three levels on Noah's ark, given the drowning waters represent hell (Gen. 6:16). How does God obviate someone just missing an A or a B? If the human race is plotted on a graph with the "y" axis being the number of people and the "x" axis representing the degree of righteousness, a continuous curve sets God up for injustice. Thus the curve is not continuous, but three distinct curves each representing a degree of glory. (Disregard those few headed for outer darkness.) In conclusion, at any point in time on the earth there are three types of people: celestial, terrestrial, and telestial, the empyrean group having the fewest numbers, because consecration is required to be celestial. This also suggests that although progression is a process, not an event, somewhere along the way we make quantum leaps.

The Church stresses to get out of debt not only because of contingencies, but interest rates on personal debt from nimiety are greater than 10 percent, which means that Latter-day Saints could pay more tithing if they became debt free first and then paid their tithing. Furthermore, if a person has more debt than assets, he or she is a liability to the Church if the United Order ushered in, even if one pays an honest tithing.

The times are ablaze with debates on abortion and the fires stoked only because people will not bridle their incontinent sex drives. The question posed by pro-abortion bellwethers is, "When does human life begin?" because the answer might let people sleep better at night. But what if it backfires? Viability of the fetus does not ring true because the age keeps decreasing with medical advances. Leviticus 17:11 states that *"the life of the flesh is in the blood,"* which first appears in the fetus at about 17 days' gestation. But what about spontaneous abortions and ones performed to spare the life of the mother? Once again, moral agency both perfected and exercised.

It is a perspicacious observation that though Joseph Smith was the modern-day Moses, it was only in spiritual outpourings, not in physical thaumaturgy. The Lord is big on recapitulations, but with a twist. This is largely for freedom protection and faith perfection. The Lord has saved the miracles like the parting of the Red Sea and the plagues for just prior to the Second Coming. There is also a strict economy on miracles in this sphere, for the Lord's retort to Lucifer when being tempted to cast Himself down from the pinnacle of the temple was, *"Thou shalt not tempt the Lord thy God."* This helps to preserve moral agency.

Recent research in psychology has documented that the personality of a child develops rapidly until age seven and then starts to taper off by age eight. This correlates well with the age of accountability, and also indicates that the parenting role is most critical early on, which is counterintuitive, since one would think that a parent could have more meaningful interaction with a child than with an infant or toddler. Yet when witnessing the acute, phatic prescience that a mother has for her infant/toddler's behavior and emotional reactions, it rings true that good parenting before age eight is a *sine qua non* in the healthy development of a child. Perhaps this is why the Lord poignantly warned, *"But whoso shall offend one of these little ones which believe in me, it were better for him that a millstone were hanged about his neck, and that he were drowned in the depth of the sea"* (Matt. 18:6). It also helps explain His declaration that the sins of the fathers are visited upon the children unto the third and fourth generation (Deut. 5:9). In summation, the God-given stewardship that we have over our children should never be taken lightly, especially early on, and the increasing number of single-parent homes is indeed a major crisis, particularly for boys (see pp. 51 and 60). Yet fortunately, God in His infinite mercy and wisdom has blessed children with an amazing resiliency.

There will always be good and evil in the universe because of moral agency, but freedom exists only because righteousness champions it by linking it to faith and responsibility. *"It is not our task to conquer all the tides of the earth, but to do what is in us to uproot evil in the fields that we know so that those who come after will have clean earth to till. What weather they shall have is not ours to tell"* (J.R.R. Tolkien).

Chapter 5
Better Living Through Chemistry

The *"Just say no!"* advice to young people today regarding drugs is precarious for two reasons. One, they witness adults improving their quality of life by "slavery" to pharmaceuticals, which confirms that there is some validity to the aphorism, *better living through chemistry*. Two, if and when they do experiment with drugs and feel the frisson, they logically conclude that their parents or teachers lied to them, or are ignorant, even if there is a hangover. These reasons only feed their defiance, which is often born after discovering how human their parents really are, or how sick society is.

The expedient course of action as guardians of our children is first to understand what they are feeling inside before they turn to drugs, and help them identify those feelings and then transform them (see chapter 1). Second, we need to admit to our children that sobriety can be dysphoric and the artificial high is indeed euphoric, but teach them that it is a "well without water." This is because it is fake, fugacious, requires drugs and enslaves the user unnecessarily to them. Moreover drugs have side effects, including nasty, inevitable withdrawals that pierce with much sorrow (1 Tim. 6:9), and dispiriting consequences such as illness and legal embroilments. Thus the only high worth having is the natural high on life, because it has none of the problems associated with the artificial one.

Finally, we must show our children that the natural high is attainable by creating, accomplishing, or producing something with hard work—especially loving relationships—or by discovering truth and increasing spirituality. Therefore although the sensation is different than the artificial high, it is actually more euphoric.

It is ironical for two reasons that members of the Church generally shun the alcoholic/addict. First, alcoholics/addicts need the Church more than anyone even though they often do not know it. People turn to mood-altering substances because they are poor in spirit. Hence another word for alcohol is "spirits." If people were rich in spirit, they would be filled with love, joy, peace, longsuffering, faith, hope, and temperance (Gal. 5:22), and they would not feel the need to use. A classic example of this is that 80 percent of Vietnam soldiers were addicted to drugs such as opiates and marijuana.

Second, one does not have to drink or use to be an alcoholic/addict. Alcoholism/addiction is an irritable state of mind where an individual does not know how to deal with personal dysphoria. It is a pervasive problem, even in the Church, because the human condition is inevitably desperate and it is only a matter of time before we all know the feeling of dysphoria. It can be a worse problem in the Church because of the pitfalls associated with attempting to live a higher law while not understanding it (see below). When Latter-day Saints do not know how to process and handle dysphoria, they may turn to mood-altering substances, but more often, they become a workaholic, or develop an addiction to food, pornography, or to a fantasy such as the superhuman condition, or a delusion such as equating selfishness to self-love, or "enabling" to love.

The key to overcoming dysphoria is summed up in the serenity prayer: *"God grant me the serenity to accept the things I cannot change, courage to change the things I can, and wisdom to know the difference."* The first step is accepting that to an extent, dysphoria is part of the plan here in mortality. This is why the first words spoken by the Lord in His Sermon on the Mount were, *"Blessed are the poor in spirit."* He knew just how daunting this life can be, and that many good people would have to endure affliction and persecution. He also knew that the most crippling handicaps were spiritual in nature, and that the broken-hearted needed Him most and would likely turn to Him. A major cause of spiritual trauma is loss of a loved one. Perhaps the best definition of youth is one who has yet to experience personal tragedy (Alfred North Whitehead). Isaiah 53:3 teaches us that the Lord was a man of sorrows acquainted with grief. Jesus taught that in this world we shall have tribulation, but He also said, *"Be of good cheer, I have overcome the world"* (John 16:33). Happiness and sorrow are not mutually exclusive on this planet. Yet peace of mind and spirit is attainable with the help of the Comforter, and godly sorrow is a deep-reaching purifier (2 Cor. 7:11) and tears a catharsis for a broken heart.

The Lord has a personal and intimate understanding of dysphoria and all of its causes including the divine dose of discontent, without which there would be no progress and we would also be too attached to the things of this world. Feeling like a stranger and a pilgrim on the earth was a confession by many saints (Heb. 11:13). They also felt the inexorable dysphoria associated with growth, and with the hunger and thirst for righteousness. *difficult*

The next step in overcoming dysphoria is to eliminate all of the unnecessary causes. There is a plethora of them including: anomie, burnout, addiction in all its forms, perfectionism, stimulus augmentation, attachment to outcomes, self-neglect, enabling, thoughts that contradict feelings (see p. 23), doing the right thing for the wrong reasons (see p. 42), lingering in the valley of decision (Joel 3:14) or in the sandbox (Neal A. Maxwell), pursuing a complete life rather than a sinless one, refusing to be comforted (Moses 7:44), denial, defiance, ingratitude, bitterness, unforgiveness, unrepentance, pessimism, hypocrisy, judging others, mixed-up priorities, and guilt or shame (see p. 21), not to mention diseases such as dysthyroidism, diabetes, obesity, etc.

Anomie means "rootlessness," and can be caused by a poor relationship with one's parents, especially the one of the same sex. This is because a father teaches a son how to be a man, not the mother, and a mother teaches a daughter how to be a woman, not the father. Another cause of anomie is the awful state of not knowing what to believe in. To truly believe in something, there has to be an understanding and a hope that it is true, regardless of opposition (Matt. 13:21). According to Alma 32, this requires fertile ground (an open heart), and nourishing (correct thinking, experience, hard work, and divine influence).

Burnout results from there being a difference between who we are and what we are doing. Burnout in a job happens when there is no passion for what one is doing, or no balance. In a church calling, burnout occurs when one is not truly converted. Burnout can be precipitated even by the minutia and grind of daily living, or by feeling possessed by our possessions. The Lord's reply to Martha's burnout was, *"There is only one thing that is needful"* (Luke 10:40–42).

Addiction is a condition that by definition requires dysfunction. Thus, one cannot be addicted to righteous living, but can be addicted to a delusion such as racial supremacy, or a fantasy surrounding the doctrine of "the chosen people." False religion can be a heady wine, and the expression *"choose your poison"* has many applications. Addictions may buy time in the short run, but because of the dysfunction associated with them, they only exacerbate dysphoria in the long run, and eventually, the addiction escalates and the situation spirals downward into a tunnel, even to the point of destruction.

The Church has its own form of dysphoria related to an attempt to live the higher law without understanding it. An example is "perfectionism," a condition not always self-inflicted, spawned from the command, *"Be ye therefore perfect"* (Matt. 5:48). It is characterized by unrealistic expectations of oneself, to the point where one feels like a failure or is unable to forgive oneself. A correct interpretation of the word *perfect* is in James 1:4: *"But let patience have her perfect work, that ye may be perfect and entire, wanting nothing."*

There are other pitfalls to the higher law. Even if perfectionism does not trip us up, we still expect more from ourselves, as does God, which predisposes us to guilt and shame. Because we are the "chosen ones," we may priggishly vaunt ourselves, or form cliques and coteries. We tend to sacralize life's small crises (a form of stimulus augmentation), or worse yet our passions, which may result in maledictions out of so-called righteous indignation. Because we have sacrificed more for the high road, we are prone to feel our love for God is unrequited when it seems we are a burlesque of previous hopes. We are more devastated by the loss of a loved one, and more likely to pray, but with insurgent tenderness, gentle deprecation, or other juvenile placations. We are more inclined to blame God and the system for failing us because we quixotically had such high expectations of it. Because of the higher stakes, we are more likely to lose our temper, and when we toss in the towel, we hurl it in and beat our chests (see *al chet*, p. 128). Heaven knows no fury like a Latter-day Saint who feels spurned (see p. 10). We must be conscious of these tendencies, and overcome them, and then help others overcome them by working to disconnect our faith from outcomes. Indeed, we would be wise to follow the example of Job who, when he lost his family, humbly replied, *"the Lord gave, and the Lord hath taken away"* (Job 1:21).

When the Lord said, *"If thy right eye offend thee then pluck it out,"* He was speaking figuratively. In other words, better to pursue a sinless life than a complete life. Better to end a friendship or change jobs (even if it means less money or prestige) if it eliminates sinister influences and sin. Better to not watch TV or movies if they undermine spirituality (J.R. Dummelow).

Many times we start feeling better and flying straight simply by looking for the good in others and forgiving without exception, including ourselves. Letting wrongs moil up inside us will cause dysphoria. Forgiveness is attainable. The Lord teaches, *"Vengeance is mine, saith the Lord,"* *"Love your enemies,"* and *"I the Lord will forgive whom I will forgive, but of you it is required to forgive all men"* (D&C 64:10), yet we know He hates iniquity (Heb. 1:9), and destroys the wicked with floods, fire, famine, plagues, and the sword, but the point is that it is the Lord's prerogative, not ours. Both the Lord and Stephen set the perfect example. When the Lord was nailed to the cross, He said, *"Father, forgive them, for they know not what they do,"* and when Stephen was stoned, he said, *"Lord, lay not this sin to their charge"* (Acts 7:60).

Pessimism can be overcome by recognizing that problems are the seeds of opportunity, and God's strength is made perfect in weakness (2 Cor. 12:9). A sense of humor does not hurt either: who likes the saturnine outlook on life? Moreover, the diversity of responses to adversity is impressive—for example, one may graciously lose an eye and then pierce the veil, while another may wind up almost 20/20 and yet still seek legal action.

There is a distinct difference between selfishness and self-love. The two greatest commandments are to love God and love your neighbor as well as yourself. What good are we to others if we do not take care of ourselves? Self-love only turns to selfishness if the attention to our own wellness is at the expense of others. Thus overall, we should give more than we receive. Celestial people are givers: they cheerfully give all they have without solicitation (2 Cor. 9:7).

In 2 Nephi 2:25 it states, *"Men are that they might have joy."* It has been said that the *j* in joy stands for Jesus, the *o* stands for others, and the *y* stands for yourself. But notice that the *j* is first, the *o* is second, and the *y* is last. If we think and act accordingly, we will escape the strictures of selfishness and find joy. Jesus gives us the formula for true success: *"But seek ye first the Kingdom of God and His righteousness; and all these things shall be added unto you"* (Matt. 6:33).

Also related is the vogue concept of "enabling," which is the reinforcement of bad behavior. We do not love people when we "enable" them. The oxymoron *tough love* is sometimes expedient.

The quiddity of all of this is that over time, learning to do the right thing for the right reasons improves the biochemical milieu in the brain to the extent that dysphoria can be overcome, and so the converse of the title of this chapter is actually a superior expression: *better chemistry through better living.* Ponce De Leon sought the *Fountain of Youth,* a fantasy spawned by twisting the true doctrine regarding the *Fountain of Living Waters* (Jer. 2:13; John 4:14; 1 Ne. 11:25). Similarly, the fantasy of alchemy as the "elixir of life" emerged from *al* (Hebrew for God) saying *"cumi"* when He raised Jairus' daughter from the dead (Mark 5:41). Consequently, Milton wrote, *"Four speedy cherubim put to their mouths the sounding alchemy";* and Shakespeare wrote, *"Gilding pale streams with heavenly alchemy."* What Ponce De Leon and those seeking alchemy did not realize is that the Melchizedek priesthood is what they were looking for, and since it had not been restored yet, they never found it because it could not be found.

There really is no excuse for Latter-day Saints to murmur about the Word of Wisdom, which is not only salubrious, but also relatively undemanding compared to the dietary code that saints had to follow when the law of Moses was in effect. The Nephites obeyed the law of Moses even after it had become dead to them (2 Ne. 25:25). Besides, if Latter-day Saints knew what was coming down the pike before the Second Coming, they would understand better that the Word of Wisdom is for their protection, not punishment. We will need every advantage to weather upcoming calamities. For example, social drinking may not cause cirrhosis, but it predisposes the liver to cirrhosis in the face of another insult such as with biological or chemical warfare, or nuclear fallout. This is why the inverse of the title, *better dying through chemistry*, may be more of a truism than the title, not to mention all the deaths solely related to DUI and drug abuse.

Another example of "better dying through chemistry" is that the top human predators use biochemical warfare. Snakes, insects, spiders, scorpions, and jellyfish are responsible for 90 percent of all human deaths from animal attacks. In fact snakes alone kill about 100,000 people every year while marauding lions kill less than 100 people every year (*Discovery Channel* and *Animal Planet*).

Yet there are other reasons why drinking is at least a mockery (Prov. 20:1). Without fail, alcohol causes a high-amplitude/short-duration depression of the central nervous system followed by a low-amplitude/long-duration agitation: there is no escaping the fuddle of the disinhibition or the lippitude of the hangover. Caffeine on the other hand, is actually a mild "speed," and consequently, it is an addictive stimulant, which on cessation, causes headaches and dysphoria. Besides, the tannins in coffee are carcinogenic.

Overlapping

Judaism
with
Mormonism

Chapter 6

The Nature of God

Much of what has been revealed about the nature of God came through His direct interactions with prophets, particularly those who started new dispensations. Joseph Smith was called at the tender age of 14, but this is not unprecedented. Samuel was a child when he received his call, and so was Jeremiah (1:6); in the Hebrew it states that Jeremiah was a *naar*, meaning "a foolish or inexperienced one." Also, Solomon was in his twenties when he was anointed king by the high priest and constructed and dedicated the temple. Ergo, the young age is not surprising for Jews. Joseph Smith revealed that Enoch was 25 years old when Adam ordained him to the patriarchal order (D&C 107:48), and Mormon was only ten years old when he received his call (Morm. 1:2).

When Joseph Smith received his call, both Elohim and Jehovah appeared to him with bodies. For some odd reason, the Jews believe that God is incorporeal, yet they would admit that Moses encountered God vis-à-vis, and ironically, the Hebrew Bible supports that indeed God does have a body. In fact, almost every part of God's body is mentioned in their Bible. These parts include: face, eyes, ears, lips, mouth, finger, hand, feet, back, thigh, and loins (Gen. 32:25; Ex. 24:9–11; 33:20–23; Num. 6:25; 12:8; Deut. 9:10; Dan. 5:5; Isa. 11:1–5; Ezek. 8:1–3).

Even God's teeth may be mentioned in the Hebrew Bible, but the Jews do not know it. The name *Sinai* could have been originally *Shinai*. *Shin* means "tooth" (*shinaim* means "teeth"), and *ai* is short for Elohim and Jehovah since the first letter of Elohim (אלהים) is *aleph*, and the first letter of Jehovah (יהוה) is *yod*. (It is more than happenstance that the word for love in Japanese is *ai*, for the Japanese are descendants of Japheth, a son of Noah, who spoke the Adamic language.) So *Shinai* literally means "the teeth of Elohim and Jehovah," and figuratively "the smile of Elohim and Jehovah." It must have been quite a sight to see Elohim and Jehovah smile at the solemn assembly recorded in Exodus 24 (also Deut. 9:10), for the mountain on which it occurred was named after it. But the Jews may have changed *Shinai* to *Sinai* because they do not believe God has a body.

Also woven into the fabric of Judaism is the spurious philosophy that there is only one God and no Godhead. This pervasive ideology is spawned from Deuteronomy 6:4, *"Shma Yisrael Adonoi Elohanu, Adonoi Echod (Hear oh Israel, the Lord our God is one*

Lord)," which is not only spoken in the synagogue, but also posted inside the synagogue and on the entry wall outside. Yet, the Hebrew Bible not only mentions *Ruach* (Holy Spirit), but also the names *Elohim* and *Jehovah*. For those with English Bibles, wherever the Torah states *Jehovah* in the Hebrew, the English translation is "Lord," and whenever the Torah has *Elohim* in the Hebrew, it is translated "God," and in the English where it says "Lord God," *Jehovah* and *Elohim* are both present in the Torah. (Joseph Smith followed suit when he translated Ether 3:6, for the brother of Jared saw the Lord *Jehovah*.)

The Jews rationalize that the names *Elohim* and *Jehovah* are for the same God who is considered to be a *ruach* (spirit), and which name was used depended on the author. But not only were there individual authors that used both names in their writing, often the names were used simultaneously in the same sentence. If both names were for the same God and used together, it would be a redundancy. In order to sort this out, let us start from the very beginning of the Bible.

Believe it or not, only the first word of the Hebrew Bible is needed to crack the case and solve the mystery, and God probably intended it that way. Joseph Smith uncannily knew this, and when he gave the King Follett Sermon, he ingeniously disentangled the skein of Jewish belief on the subject. In the eulogy, Joseph put the Hebrew Bible's first word *Borashes* (בראשית) which figuratively means "in the beginning," in Hebraic dishabille by explaining that a Jew without any authority added the *beth* (ב) and that the last two letters (ית) are a grammatical ending.

Nevertheless, it is high time someone picked up the ball and expanded the explanation. The root word is *rosh*, meaning "head," the *beth* (ב) means "in," and the ית (i,t) is the *–ite* suffix and indicates a descendant and/or follower, as in Israelite, Nephite, Lamanite, and so on. A classic example of this is the word בעברית, which means *in Hebrew*. If the *beth* and the last two letters are dropped, the remaining word is *Eber*, who is the father of the Hebrews who are also "Eberites."

So it should be clear that the first word of the Hebrew Bible literally means the "Head's descendants who follow the Head," or "Godites of the Godites." In other words, it is not good enough just to be a descendant, one has to follow too, and this is why Paul calls himself *"an Hebrew of the Hebrews"* (Philip. 3:5). The concept of a Godite is not unprecedented in the Hebrew Bible for Genesis 6:2 mentions the sons of Elohim who are "Godites." Yet if we zoom in on the Hebrew letters in *Roshes*, which is actually a beautiful cryptogram, its full meaning blossoms forth. Once again, the *aleph* (א) signifies Elohim (אלהים) since the first letter in Elohim is *aleph*. Elohim is facing the reader, and to His left is the *resh* (ר), which represents the Holy Ghost since in Hebrew, *Ruach* (רוח) is "Holy Spirit." To Elohim's right is a *shaddai yod* (ש י—the *shin* is short for *shaddai*) which means "almighty Jehovah" since *shaddai* means "almighty" and *yod* is the first letter of Jehovah (יהוה). Notice the consistency of Jehovah standing on the right hand of God (Acts 7:55–56).

What about the *tau* (ת)? Because it is the last letter in the Hebrew alphabet, it is symbolic of *the end*. The *aleph* also represents *the beginning* since it is the first letter of the Hebrew alphabet. Notice that the *Almighty Jehovah, who is Alpha and Omega, the beginning and the end* (Rev. 1:8, 11; 21:6; 22:13; 3 Ne. 9:18; D&C 19:1; 38:1; 45:7), is in between the *aleph* and the *tau* in *Roshes* (ראשית). A perfect fit!

As an informative aside, when Joseph Smith translated 3 Nephi 9:18, it probably read את on the Gold Plates. The translation was the Greek *Alpha and Omega* rather than the English "A and Z" because the world understood the Greek better than the English or the Hebrew (Rev. 1:8, 11; 21:6; 22:13).

In summation, the first word of the Hebrew Bible means the "Godhead comprising Elohim, Jehovah, and the *Ruach,* and God's obedient descendants." (Notice how one Hebrew word can mean so much in English.) This contradicts the Jewish belief in the nature of God, but fits perfectly Joseph Smith's conception. It only gets worse for the Jews and better for the Latter-day Saints as the sentence continues. The next word is *bora* meaning "to create or organize." Thus the Godhead and God's obedient descendants created (organized). This is exactly what Joseph Smith taught—that we are God's spirit children and we helped create the earth. The temple teaches that Michael, who is Adam, was Jehovah's right-hand man when the earth was created.

Since the first word of the Bible was originally *Roshes* meaning the "Godhead and God's obedient descendants," or *Borashes* meaning literally "in the Godhead and God's obedient descendants," it follows that the title of *Genesis* should be "The Godhead and God's obedient Descendants," and *Genesis* is a manmade erroneous title. The complete title of the book of Genesis should be, "The Godhead and God's obedient Descendants Create, and the Patriarchal Order." The book would be subdivided by dispensation: the dispensations of Adam, Enoch, and Noah, and the dispensation of the gospel of Abraham through Melchizedek, who is also Eber.

What are the correct names for the other five books of Moses? A better name than *Exodus* is "Passover" since the universe revolves around the Atonement. *Leviticus* should be "Aaronicus" (see p. 106) or better yet, "The Aaronic Order." *Numbers* should be *Leviticus*, or even better, "The Levitical Order." A superior name to *Deuteronomy* would be "The Law of Moses Repeated."

If there is any shred of doubt on what has been revealed here concerning the first word of the Hebrew Bible, it is corroborated by the first sentence of the Hebrew Bible, which directly and/or cryptogrammatically reiterates the members of the Godhead. It specifically mentions Elohim (God the Father) and *Ruach* (Holy Ghost), but hidden in the grammar is also Jehovah. After *"Borashes bora,"* the Hebrew states, *"Elohim ET ha shemayim va ET ha oretz,"* meaning *"God created the heaven and the earth."* The Hebrew particle *et* (את) indicates the defined direct object, and cannot be translated in the English since there is no word for it in English. Lo and behold, it also signifies Jehovah, since aleph and tau are the first and last letters of the Hebrew alphabet and typify *the beginning and the end*, another name for Jehovah. The beauty of the direct object particle being Jehovah is that Elohim created the earth through Jehovah; in fact, everything that

Chapter 6 – The Nature of God

happens definitively is through Jehovah. In summation, Elohim was the master architect, Jehovah was the general contractor, and Elohim's other children were the sub-contractors and laborers. *that is you + me!*

Comparatively, in Japanese the accusative or objective case is indicated by the particle *o*, which has a quiescent *w* and corresponds to ו in Hebrew. Thus even in Japanese, all action goes through Jehovah since ו is another token of Jehovah (see pp. 135–136).

Further evidence of this hidden meaning in the direct object grammar is in the Hebrew of Genesis 24:7, which this time reveals who the *ET* is. It starts *"Jehovah Elohi ha Shemayim,"* which is the same as *"Elohim ET ha Shemayim."*

Another example in the Hebrew Bible where the members of the Godhead are listed cryptogrammatically is in Daniel chapter 5 where the finger of God writes *mina, mina, tekel, upharsin* on the wall. It is interesting that Daniel, a good Jewish priesthood holder, immediately knew the meaning, while it baffled the Babylonians. Daniel realized instantly that the three members of the Godhead were encrypted in the writing. The first *a* (א) is an abbreviation for Elohim since Elohim starts with *aleph* (א). The second *a* (א) and the *t* (ת) in *tekel* signify Jehovah, since He is *Alpha and Omega, the beginning and the end.* Notice that Jehovah is again to Elohim's right, but this time their backs are to Babylon in repudiation. The *u* (ו) in *upharsin* is the token of the Holy Ghost since the Hebrew for "Holy Ghost" is *Ruach* (רוח), which has the *u* (ו) in it, and the Hebrew for "Persia" is *Pharsin* that does not have a *u* in it. The reason the Holy Ghost is to Jehovah's right is because the Godhead was showing the Father, the Son, and the Holy Ghost, in that order. Another way to look at this sentence is that the Godhead called to Persia, since the *kol* in *tekel* means "voice," just as the *kol* in *Kolob*, which means the "voice of Father." The English word *rue*, which means "godly sorrow and repentance," comes from the Hebrew *Ruach* (Holy Ghost), who engenders godly sorrow, repentance, and new *life* (חיים).

As a related aside, the first author had a mission president in Japan named *Ushio*. He never knew the meaning of his unusual name, but it actually is the sacred Hebrew cryptogram ושיו: the ו is the token of the Holy Ghost, and the שיו means "the almighty Jehovah who creates." Thus *Ushio* in Hebrew means "the Holy Ghost and the almighty Jehovah who creates." Once again, this is compelling evidence that Japanese evolved from the Adamic language.

Given that the ו is the token of the Holy Ghost, it is imperative that we return to the first line in the Hebrew Bible and reconsider the *vav* (ו), which is used in Hebrew for the conjunction *and*. If it is pronounced *oo* instead of *va*, it cryptogrammatically indicates the *Ruach*. So once again, the Holy Ghost is cryptogrammatically in the first sentence of the Bible. It is metaphorical that the copula *and* can signify the Holy Ghost, who functions as the "glue" for the Godhead.

The first line of the Hebrew Bible is so beautiful in the way it is constructed, it was probably written by God Himself. This also rings true because in order to be an author of Genesis, one had to be an eyewitness of the events recorded. Moreover, Elohim was the only

74

one with a body when the creation commenced (other than mother in heaven). The original Hebrew is the Adamic language, which will be spoken in the millenium (Zeph. 3:9).

Not only are all the members of the Godhead in the first word and line of Genesis, they continue to be present throughout the first chapter. Genesis 1:26 states, "and *God* [Elohim] said let *us* make man in *our* image." The rabbis reason that God was including the angels. The Jews are so hidebound as to Exodus 20:3, *"thou shalt have no other gods before me,"* that they are confused: idolatry was so suffusive an evil in ancient Israel that the Jews have overcorrected.

The second chapter of Genesis starts with Elohim, but then mentions Jehovah in the fifth verse. In chapter three, they are both present but Jehovah is mentioned first. By chapter four, Elohim has departed from the scene on the earth and left His perfect protégé Jehovah in charge. Thus Genesis from the start and throughout is in harmony with Joseph Smith having seen two personages. Yet the evidence continues to mount elsewhere in the Torah.

Although Elohim leaves the scene, He appears again every once in a while, but not for a mere exercise on appearances. The truth is that Elohim is always present when a new dispensation is started: Gen. 1–3—Adam; Gen. 5:24—Enoch; Gen. 6:9—Noah; Gen. 17:1–7—Abraham; Ex. 24—Moses. Even in Deuteronomy 9:10, it states that Jehovah gave Moses two stone tablets written by the finger of Elohim, suggesting once again that there is a Godhead with more than one God. This was exactly Joseph Smith's experience in the (sacred) grove near Palmyra, NY when he ushered in the dispensation of the fullness of times.

Other indications of the Godhead in Genesis that the Jews do not even consider are the origin of the name *Abel*, and the commandment to offer blood sacrifice. Adam knew Elohim personally, and to honor Him, he named one of his sons *Abel*, meaning "God the Father" (*ab* means "father," *el* means "God"). Also, Elohim commanded Adam and his sons to offer immolation in similitude of the sacrifice of His Only Begotten Son, Jehovah, another member of the Godhead. This all lends credence to the concept of a Godhead. (The expression, *you can't squeeze blood out of a turnip,* comes from the chiding Cain received from Abel for offering a bloodless sacrifice of turnips.)

Another possible discrepancy in the Hebrew Bible related to this specious reasoning by the Jews that there is only one God is that Elohim is sometimes spelled without a *mem*. When Jesus was on the cross, He said, *"Eloi, Eloi lama sabachthani"* (Mark 15:34). At first glance, this would imply that *Elohi* is another correct name for Elohim. But Psalms 22:1 and Matthew 27:46 give the proper Hebrew: *"Eli, Eli lama sabachthani?"* *Eloi* is a Greek rendition of *Eli*, and therefore, *Elohi* could be an error in the Hebrew Bible, and the *mem* may have been left off because it connotes plurality of Gods. The only other explanation is that the authors, out of reverence, did not use the complete name, which is sacred.

The reverse error of mentioning Elohim when He was not around also occurs in the Hebrew Bible. In 1 Samuel 28:13, it says that Elohim appeared to Saul and the Witch of En-dor, which is a mistranslation. There is no ostensible reason for Elohim to appear not only to a witch, but also to a murderer of 85 priests of God, including the high priest *Ahimelech* (1 Sam. 22:18). It should read *elim*, meaning "false gods."

Joseph Smith also hit a grand slam on this very subject when he corrected Malachi 4:2. In the English it says "sun," which is the correct translation of the Hebrew, which says *shemesh*. Malachi is quoted in 3 Nephi 25:2, but it states, *"Son of righteousness"* instead of *"Sun of righteousness."* Since the Jews believe there is one God, they changed *Son* to *Sun*. So once again, even the Hebrew Bible has errors.

Here is yet another fascinating overlap on the nature of God that is a feather in Joseph Smith's prophetic hat. The Star of David is an icon for the Jews. They purport that it represents the interaction between God and man. The triangle with the apex down betokens God looking down on man, and the other triangle typifies man looking up to God. Joseph Smith comes along and strategically places the Star of David on the temple with a Holy of Holies, the only place on the planet where God communicates vis-à-vis with man. Furthermore, the Jews do not believe in a Godhead, but Joseph Smith preached that there was a Godhead with three members. The triangle in the Star of David representing God has three corners for those three members. The Jews have not had a prophet for 2400 years, but The Church of Jesus Christ of Latter-day Saints has a prophet with two counselors who fit perfectly into the corners of the other triangle pointing up to God (Hartman Rector Jr.). In summation, Joseph Smith had a better understanding of the meaning of the Star of David than the Jews do.

A related enigma is the origin of '' (*the Word*). Perhaps the greatest motivations for the Israelites to create a pseudonym for Jehovah were an implacable determination not to take His name in vain, and various persecutions like those endured during the Babylonian captivity where Jews were threatened with death if found worshipping Jehovah rather than Nebuchadnezzar's god (Dan. 3). The second *yod* is either an honorific suffix (as in the sacred parlance *Adonoi*) and/or a substitute for the *vav* in Jehovah (Gesenius' *Hebrew-Chaldee Lexicon to the Old Testament* under *Adonoi* and *Vav*). Now when John the Revelator writes "In the beginning was *the Word*" (John 1:1), and, "Our hands have handled *the Word* of life" (1 Jn. 1:1), and, "Bear record in heaven, the Father, *the Word,* and the Holy Ghost" (1 Jn. 5:7), the Greeks called '' "*the Word*" because either they did not know the meaning, or they did not want to insult the Jews by using the name *Jehovah.*

The pseudonym '' also appears in other places—for example, Hawaii and Sawaii in Samoa: the Polynesians are of the house of Israel, and in anticipation of the Lord's second coming, they inserted '' at the end of the names of the main islands. Moreover, God in Samoan is *Tama alii*: the *al* is short for Elohim, and the '' signifies Jehovah. Finally, *ii* in Japanese means "good," as does *yoi* ('''). Contradistinctively, *wŏrui* in Japanese means "bad," and in Hebrew it means "evil spirit." The implications of '' (*the Word*) and '' (*wo*) appearing in the Japanese are almost mind-boggling. Did they come from Polynesian influence or from the Adamic language at the time of the Tower of Babel?

Chapter 7
The Stick of Joseph

After Joseph Smith's experience with the Godhead, he was given the *stick of Joseph* on Gold Plates from the hill *Cumorah*. Although Ezekiel mentions two sticks (Ezek. 37:15–16), the Jews today do not discuss it. Since Ezekiel lived about 575 B.C., there was obviously no printing press. Thus, in order to keep records, the Israelites used one of two methods. The first was to dry animal skins and write with ink or dye on the undersurface, then wrap the skin around a smooth stick to store it. The Torah in the synagogue is an example of this. The second method was to melt ore, such as gold or copper, cast the metal into flat plates and engrave the message upon the metallic plates. The first method was simpler, but the record was more vulnerable to decomposition. The second was more time consuming and the plates were heavy to transport, but they would survive the elements—for example, the Gold Plates that Joseph Smith translated.

Now when Ezekiel talked about two sticks with writing on them, he was referring to one record concerning the Jews, the Bible, (this name comes from the word *bibliography*), the other record was from the people of Joseph who received the birthright (1 Chron. 5:1–2). Both books testify of the Messiah and the Jews believe that at least two witnesses are required to establish truth (Deut. 17:6). The stick of Joseph states that a third record will come forth from the 10 lost tribes of Israel (2 Ne. 29:3–14). Thus the overlaps of Judaism by Mormonism continue.

Curiously, the Jews today never talk about Joseph receiving the birthright from Jacob, even though it is in the Hebrew Bible (Gen. 49:22–26). There it states, *"Joseph is a fruitful bough by a well whose branches run over the wall,"* meaning that Joseph's descendants will be numerous and near a body of water like an ocean that was a barrier to them, but they crossed it. It also states that Joseph's descendants will become the shepherd and the stone of Israel. A shepherd cares for the sheep and when the sheep get lost, the good shepherd goes out to find them, and this is what is happening through missionary work. Jacob also says in verse 26: *"The blessings of thy father have prevailed above the blessings of my progenitors unto the utmost bound of the everlasting hills."* The Hebrew rendition has *ad taavat givot olam,* which literally means, "till, limits, mountains, world," or in other words, has for its limits a mountain chain from one end of the world to the other. (*Ad* and *olam* together means "everlasting," but here they are separated.) Abraham and Isaac were promised the land of Canaan from the Nile to the Euphrates, but Joseph through Jacob was promised the Americas. Since America is the land of Joseph, it is most appropriate that the stick of Joseph would come out of America, just as the Bible, the stick of Judah, comes from the land of Judah, not Palestine, which means the *land of the Philistines.*

The stick of Joseph (Jacob 5) has an allegory from the book of Zenos, a lost book of the Hebrew Bible (along with Jasher) that gives a vivid description of the scattering and the gathering of Israel. When Israel fell just before 700 B.C., those who fled west of the Black Sea joined the Khumri, who became Celts. Those who were taken captive and then escaped north of the Black Sea blended in with the Scythians (Col. 3:11), who became Germanic (Dr. Terry Blodgett, SUU).

There are numerous indications of the dispersion in Europe such as Denmark means "field of Dan," and the Danes come from the tribe of Dan. Moreover, Saxon comes from Isaacson, and the Germanic name *Robert* is the mirror-image of *tre-b-or*, a Hebrew phrase read from right to left, meaning "strength in light."

Furthermore, *Brit* is Hebrew for "covenant," and *ish* means "man"; therefore, *British* means "man of the covenant." Excaliber also has a Hebrew origin: "Ex" comes from *ets* meaning "stick," and *k-eli-ber* means, "as my God creates"; so *Excaliber* means, "the stick which my God creates." The Irish shillelagh has a similar Hebrew origin: *shel* means "of" and *eli* means "my God." So the *shillelagh stick* is the "rod of my God." (See "Shillelagh Song" on p. 90.) This is strong evidence of the scattering in the British Isles.

What about the Diaspora in France? Curiously, when Joseph Smith translated the stick of Joseph, the French word *adieu* appeared through the Urim and Thummim (Jacob 7:27). Why a French word?

Because on the Gold Plates was probably the encryption אתיאו, which is transliterated *AThIEU*, or the French word *adieu* courtesy of the Hebraic sound shifts in French (see p. 18). You see, the language on the Gold Plates was reformed Egyptian (Morm. 9:32), which is Egyptian characters with Hebrew letters selectively interspersed, in the same way Japanese is Chinese characters with Hiragana, and Yiddish is German and Hebrew written in Hebrew letters. Thus there were times when to communicate perspicuously (Morm. 9:33), the authors of the Book of Mormon used only Hebrew—as in *Wo Wo Wo* (see pp. 45–46), or *adieu*. *Adieu* is French meaning "to God," yet look what happens if one solves its Hebrew cryptogram: once again, the את is Jehovah since He is *Alpha and Omega, the beginning and the end* (see pp. 71–73); the י is also Jehovah just as it is in *Borashes* (see p. 70), since *yod* is the first letter of Jehovah; the other א signifies Elohim just as in *Borashes*, since *aleph* is the first letter of Elohim; and the ו is a token of the *Ruach* or Holy Ghost (see pp. 73–74). Thus the original meaning of *adieu* was the "Godhead"—with Jehovah on Elohim's right as always, and the *Ruach* (Holy Ghost) on Elohim's left. This is a potent indication of the dispersion in France.

Further compelling evidence is the French phrase *Je suis*, meaning "I am," but it is also Jesus with a *yod* in it. The French knew from being grafted into the house of Israel that Jesus was the great "I am," so when they coined the phrase *Je suis* to mean "I am," they merely inserted a *yod* in Jesus because they knew it was a token of Jehovah, the great "I am." Moreover, the verb "to be" in French is *etre*, which is actually a transliteration of the Hebrew cryptogram אתרא: once again, *et* (את) is Jehovah since He is *Alpha and Omega, the beginning and the end*; the *resh* signifies the *Ruach* as in *Borashes*; and the second *aleph* signifies Elohim. Therefore, the verb "to be" in French is the members of the Godhead, and without them we would cease to exist.

When Joseph Smith translated the stick of Joseph, he did not know Hebrew, yet the names that he translated from the ancient records were obviously Hebrew names. For example, *Lehi* and *Nephi* are the first two names mentioned in the Book of Mormon. *Lehi* in Hebrew means "jawbone" (Judg. 15:17). The Douay version of the Holy Bible mentions the name *Nephi* in 2 Maccabees 1:36, which suggests that *Nephi* in Hebrew means "purification." This is further evidence that Joseph Smith was inspired because he did not know Hebrew when this was translated. In fact, all the names in the Book of Mormon except two have Hebrew roots. The two exceptions are Bountiful and Desolation. "Bountiful" in Hebrew is *acne* (אחני), and "desolation" in Hebrew is *shmama* (שממה). Since the Hebrew names sound crude, Joseph Smith used the English names in the translation to be more reverent and to deter criticism.

Moreover, the name *Cumorah* has a Hebrew origin: *Cum* comes from המקום meaning "the place," *or* is Hebrew for "light," and *ah* is short for Jehovah. Hence, *Cumorah* means, "the place with the light of

Jehovah." One must not make the *faux pas* that others have made of claiming that *Cumorah* comes from the Hebrew word *cumor* (כמר) which means "false priest" (2 Kgs. 23:5; Zeph. 1:4). There is no reason why the Lord would name a sacred place after the word for a false priest.

Contradistinctively, the word *cumor* is found in the name of the brother of Jared, which is *Mahonri Moriancumer* (Alma 8:7; Ether 2:13). But in this case, *cumor* is preceded by the negative אין (*ain*), which means "there is not." Thus, *Moriancumer* means, "from my light there is no false priest." The 16 stones that the Lord touched with his finger were evidence that the brother of Jared was no false priest, and therefore *Moriancumer* was added to *Mahonri*.

Furthermore, the book of Abraham states that *Kolob* is the planet nearest to God. In Hebrew, *kol* means "voice" and *ab* means "father." Hence, *Kolob* is the place where the voice of Heavenly Father is heard.

Even the word *Mormon* has Hebrew roots. *M* in front of a noun means "from," *or* is the noun in Hebrew meaning "light," and "mon" comes from the Hebrew word *man* meaning "manna" (Ex. 16:31). Thus, *Mormon* means, "manna is from the light of God." In his *Teachings of the Prophet Joseph Smith* (pp. 299–300), Joseph says that *Mormon* means "more good," since *mon* is the Egyptian word meaning "good." But how could *Mormon* come from an English word and an Egyptian word if English did not exist yet?

After Joseph Smith translated the stick of Joseph, he realized the importance of Hebrew and studied it in the School of the Prophets which was similar to Samuel's (1 Sam. 19:18–20; D&C 88:136–138), and from all information, he was a great student. For example, he called a Mormon city *Nauvoo* because he knew the Saints were only going to be there temporarily. However the Saints had just been driven out of Independence, Missouri and he did not want to discourage them further, so he told them that *Nauvoo* meant "city beautiful." But *Nauvoo* is a Hebrew word meaning "we will come temporarily." During the exodus, when Moses took the children of Israel to a temporary campsite, the Torah says *ya vaoo* which means "they came temporarily" (Ex. 15:27; 19:1–2). Similarly, Joseph Smith took the Saints to a temporary location and called it *Nauvoo*, which means "we will come temporarily." He would have called it *Nashvoo* if they were staying permanently.

Without getting too far afield, here are some other insights from the Hebrew: Utah is the state of Judah, which means "praise Jehovah"; *Arizona* in Hebrew means, "the lion of Zion is Jehovah"; *Oregon* is Hebrew for "my light is a garden"; *Nevada* is Hebrew for "we will serve Jehovah"; and *Idaho* is Hebrew for "the hand of Jehovah creates." Even California comes from Hebrew: *Caliph* means clap, *or* means "light," *ni* means "birth," and *ah* comes from Jehovah. Thus *California* means "a clap of thunder and lightning is the birth of Jehovah." This shows that the American Indians had Hebrew roots, which corroborates Joseph

Smith as a true prophet since the Book of Mormon indicates that its people migrated from Jerusalem around 600 B.C.

Similarly, Alaska and Hawaii are acronyms of Hebrew words, and it was the Lord's will that they be incorporated into the United States of America. This is because Alaskans and Hawaiians are descendants of Joseph, and Joseph inherited the land of America (see above). With the name *Alaska*, *al* means "God," *ash* means "fire" (the English word *ash* is the product of the Hebrew word *ash*) and *k-ah* means "like Jehovah." Therefore, *Alaska* means literally, "the fire of God is like Jehovah," or figuratively, "the Spirit of God like a fire is burning."

As for *Hawaii*, *ha* means "behold," *va* (בא) means "to come," and *ii* (יי) is the pseudonym for Jehovah (see p. 78). Hence, *Hawaii* means "behold, Jehovah is to come." Moreover, the greeting from the Hawaiians is *aloha* which comes from the Hebrew: *al* means "God," *o* means "to create," and *ah* comes from Jehovah; therefore *aloha* means, "Jehovah is the God who creates." Furthermore, *cahunah* is the Hawaiian word for "priest," and *cahunah* in Hebrew literally means "priest of Jehovah," and figuratively "priesthood." Finally, the Hawaiian guitar or *ukulele* is Hebrew for "the voice of my God Jehovah." The stick of Joseph mentions that a man named *Hagoth* built a very large ship and sailed west of America toward the South Pacific islands (Alma 63:5). This all corroborates the authenticity of the Book of Mormon.

Another overlap of the stick of Judah and the stick of Joseph is the use of the term *Zion*. Acronyms exist in Hebrew as well as in English, and *Zion* is one of them. The *z* comes from *zedek* (as in *Melchizedek*) meaning "righteousness," the *i* comes from the first letter (*yod*) of Jehovah, the *o* is a ו meaning "He creates" (see p. 136), and the *n* comes from the word *ne-aman* meaning "faithful forever." Thus *Zion* means "righteousness that Jehovah creates is faithful forever."

Moreover, the Hebrew acronym *amen* is used in both sticks and comes from the first letter of three Hebrew words: *emmett* (אמת) meaning "truth," *mayatah* (מעתה) meaning "from now," and *ne-aman* (נאמן) meaning "forever." Therefore, *amen* means "truth is from now and forever," and this is why we use the word *amen* when we close our prayers in the name of Jesus Christ, who is Jehovah and the author of all truth.

The word *amen* has been erroneously inserted in place of the name *Ahman* (Rev. 3:14). Joseph Smith revealed that Jehovah is son *Ahman* (D&C 78:20; 95:17), who established the foundations of Adam-ondi-Ahman (D&C 78:15; 107:53). *Ahman* is amen with an *h* in it from Jehovah. Therefore, *Ahman* means, "truth is from now and forever through Jehovah." In *Mormon Doctrine* under the subtitle "Ahman," McConkie says that *Ahman* is God the Father since the "man" in *Ahman* comes from "Man of Holiness." With all due respect, it is obvious that Elder McConkie did not know Hebrew, and he made the same mistake with *Ahman* that Joseph Smith made with *Mormon* (see p. 84)—namely, the assumption that a Hebrew word's transliteration has the same meaning as the English word that matches it. If *Ahman* were God the Father, then D&C 78:20 and 95:17 should read "son **of** *Ahman*," but notice the *of* is missing.

The predominant understanding of the word *ondi* is that it means "report," since that is the meaning of the French word *on dit* (quiescent t), which has become an English word. But *ondi* in Adam-ondi-Ahman comes from the Hebrew and means "power sufficient": *on* (און) means "power" and *di* (די) means "sufficient." Thus *Adam-ondi-Ahman* means "Adam and his righteous posterity have power sufficient through Jehovah." The name *Moroni* means "from light is my power"; notice that it has the word *on* in it. The Ande(s) mountain range may have been named after this word *ondi*.

Another acronym related to Zion is the Hebrew word *zohar* coined by Elohim. In Genesis 6:16, God commands Noah to put a *zohar* in the ark. But Noah asked, "What is a *zohar*?" God explained that Noah could look to Mount Zion, or the City of Enoch, or the place where God dwells, through a window in the ark. Thus the Hebrew word for window is *zohar*, a similitude of Mount Zion: the *zo* comes from *Zion* and *har* is Hebrew for "mountain." *Har* has been transliterated into the English as *ar*—for example, Armageddon comes from *Har-Meggido* and Arrarat comes from *Har-Oret* meaning, "the mountain with the light of

Jehovah." (Obviously, when Noah coined the name, he knew what *et* (את) meant.)

Both sticks (Nephi and Isaiah) discuss Mount Zion or the New Jerusalem (D&C 84:1–4). The stick of Joseph also mentions that there will be a New Jerusalem in America (3 Ne. 20:22) where Adam and Eve and the City of Enoch existed, and Noah's ark was built just prior to the deluge/noyade. Adam will return to Adam-ondi-Ahman in Missouri, the City of Enoch will return to the Gulf of Mexico, and Noah's ark will be put in the reliquary called "The Lord's Museum" in the New Jerusalem with a sign next to it stating, "Is anything too hard for the Lord?" Independence, Missouri is 800 miles from the Gulf of Mexico, but since Revelation 21:16 states that the New Jerusalem will be over 1300 miles long, the two locations could be part of the same city.

When Joseph Smith established the Church, he instituted the ordinance of the sacrament the same way it was practiced in the stick of Joseph. The Jews do not have such an ordinance, but the Torah mentions it. In Genesis 14:18 it states that Melchizedek brought forth bread and wine. Until August 1830, The Church of Jesus Christ of Latter-day Saints used bread and wine as sacramental emblems, but D&C 27 states that a heavenly messenger instructed Joseph Smith to use water instead of wine for a sacramental emblem. When Moses, Aaron, Nadab, Abihu, and 70 elders of Israel came into the presence of God, it states in Exodus 24:11, *"And they did eat and drink."* It was not pretzels and zythum at a Monday Night Football game; it was the emblems of the sacrament.

Joseph Smith also revealed the Word of Wisdom, a dietary code less stringent than that of the law of Moses. In D&C 89, Latter-day Saints are admonished to eschew wine, among other things. At the Passover Seder, it is customary to drink wine, yet the Passover manual states that the drink should be *preehagofen,* which is non-fermented grape juice. *Yayin,* which is Hebrew for "wine," is not mentioned, yet Jews simper over their wine at Passover.

Shillelagh Song

Oh, fifty years ago
me father left old Erin shore,
He landed here shillelagh in hand
and divell a penny more.

He got a job, and got a wife,
and then a family,
and when he died he left
his old shillelagh stick with me.

Sure 'tis the same old shillelagh
me father could lick a dozen men,
As fast as they'd get up be gory
he'd knock 'em right down again.

And many's the time he used it on me
to make me understand,
Sure 'tis the same old shillelagh
me father brought from Ireland.

Chapter 8

The Urim and Thummim and the Aaronic Order

The overlaps of Judaism and Mormonism pertaining to the Urim and Thummim and the Aaronic priesthood are so rich and plentiful that they alone substantiate Joseph Smith as a true prophet. This is not to mention the irony that he knew much more about the interpreters with Hebrew origin than the Jews do, or than he expressed to know. Even so, it is understandable given he actually used them, and was instructed on how to use them, yet strictly forbidden to reveal explicit details concerning such, because of their sacred nature. Alas, apostasy results in the revocation of sacred things, and their true meaning and function being twisted, diluted, or lost, while a dearth of faith keeps it that way.

If the reader wonders why the authors linked the interpreters with the Aaronic order, it is because the terminology *Urim* (אורים) and *Thummim* (תמים) and Aaron's priesthood office of *cohen* (כהן), which means "priest of Aaron," first appear in the Bible together in Exodus 28. Moreover, only the high priest (כהן גדול), who held the keys of that priesthood (כהנה), had the legal right to wear and use the Urim and Thummim: Moses and Joshua were the prophets, but the sacred *lots* were worn and operated by Aaron and Eleazar (Ex. 28:30, 43; Num. 27:21).

Yet Joseph Smith revealed that both the priesthood and the interpreters existed prior to that time. The lesser priesthood of God holds the keys of baptism, repentance, and the ministering of angels (D&C 13), and was on the earth throughout the book of Genesis as an appendage to the greater priesthood (D&C 107:14), else how could Adam and his descendants have been baptized by authority (Moses 6:64), and Noah (Elias—D&C 27:7) have overseen the baptism of the earth?

As for the Urim and Thummim, Aaron received them from Moses, who discovered them along with the record of Genesis when he extirpated Joseph's remains from Egypt (Ex. 13:19). How did Joseph get them? Abraham had the Urim and Thummim (Abr 3:1), and bequeathed them to Isaac, who in turn gave them to Jacob. Abraham received them from Melchizedek (Eber) who inherited them from Shem along with the record of Genesis (Gen. 10:21). This would imply that Moses abridged Genesis in the same way Mormon abridged the Book of Mormon (see *Authors of Genesis* by Irving H. Cohen, located in the BYU library).

Melchizedek and the brother of Jared were contemporaries because they both lived at the time of the Tower of Babel. This suggests that the brother of Jared had a separate Urim and Thummim given to him on the mount when he saw the finger of the Lord touch 16 other stones (D&C 17:1). Shortly after the flood, the continents were divided (Gen. 10:25), so there was need for another Urim and Thummim, Aaron's for the land of Judah, the brother of Jared's for the land of Joseph (Mosiah 8:13).

When Moses bestowed the Urim and Thummim on Aaron in Exodus 28, the Israelites had not yet blown their chances for the higher law and priesthood, and the government of the church closely mirrored the one Joseph Smith established: Moses was the president and his two counselors were Joshua and Aaron; there were 12 princes (Num. 17:2, 6) presiding over the 12 tribes, analogous to The Quorum of the Twelve Apostles; there were 70 elders of Israel (Ex. 24:1,9; Num. 11:16–17) composing the first quorum of the Seventy; and finally, Aaron and his sons constituted the Presiding Bishopric, and according to Exodus (28:43; 29:9; 30:21; 40:15), they had legal right to the office forever which included the use of the Urim and Thummim (see also D&C 68:16–18; 107:16). The Jews today are not only oblivious to the full meaning and functions of the Urim and Thummim, but also church government comprising The Quorum of the Twelve, the first quorum of the Seventy, and the Presiding Bishopric, even though all of this is substantiated by the Torah. Even the word *quorum* comes from Hebrew: *que* (קוה) means "to hope" and *rum* (רום) means "to edify," so *quorum* means "to hope and edify." Notice that *quorum* has a double dose of the Holy Ghost (ו). Also, the term *Qumran* may be related to the word *quorum: Qumran* may have been originally *que-m-rum* meaning "hope from on high."

It is important to clarify that although the high priest, which in Hebrew is *cohen gadol*, held the keys of the lesser priesthood, he himself had the Melchizedek priesthood, in the same way bishops today hold the keys of the Aaronic priesthood while being Melchizedek priesthood holders. By definition a high priest must hold the Melchizedek priesthood (Heb. 5:6, 10; 6:20; 7:15, 21), and in order to hold priesthood keys, even those of the Aaronic priesthood, one must be a Melchizedek priesthood holder.

Another indication that the high priest or *cohen gadol* held the greater priesthood is that he was the only priest (*cohen*) allowed into the Holy of Holies, or into the presence of God, which requires the Melchizedek priesthood (D&C 84:22). Indeed Aaron, the first *cohen gadol*, held the Melchizedek priesthood, for he came into the presence of God on Mount Sinai (Ex. 24:9–10). The high priest (*cohen gadol*) would receive the Melchizedek priesthood from the prophet living at the time.

An unfortunate misconception by many Latter-day Saints is that John the Baptist, a *cohen gadol*, did not hold the Melchizedek priesthood. But indeed he did and probably was ordained by the Lord sometime after he baptized the Lord. If the Savior refers to John the Baptist as more than a prophet and the greatest man born of woman up to that point in time other than Himself (Matt. 11:9–11), then certainly it follows that John the Baptist was a Melchizedek priesthood holder.

Although the world does not consider John the Baptist's father, Zacharias, to have been a high priest (*cohen gadol*), he probably was, or at least could/should have been. In Luke 1:5–25, the most likely occasion at hand was the annual Day of Atonement (*Yom ha Kippurim*), which requires the presence and priesthood authority of the high priest. This would make Zacharias the high priest *quoad sacra,* since Simon son of Boëthus, Herod's appointed high priest was on the verge of being deposed (FF Bruce's *New Testament History*). Why would *"the whole multitude of the people"* wait for Zacharias if he were not the high priest officiating that day (Luke 1:10, 21)? Although Luke 1:5 states that Zacharias was a priest of the course of Abia (Abijah), this does not exclude him from being a high priest (Lev. 16:30–32; Num. 27:21; 1 Chron. 24:6; Ps. 110:4; 1 Maccabees 14:41; Heb 5:6; 7:21). Sometimes the terms *priest* and *high priest* are used interchangeably in the scriptures. Moreover, neither the Maccabean high priests nor Herod's high priests were Zadokite, and Herod's were imposters—perhaps at times even titular—for they were only in office via corruption. Trumping all this is the fact that Gabriel appears and makes his announcement, confirming that Zacharias was indeed God's high priest.

Furthermore, Luke 1:9 says that Zacharias burned incense, which originally was the responsibility of the high priest (Ex. 30:7). Luke 1:9 also mentions the word *lot,* which is a strong indication that the Urim and Thummim were extant (see p. 102) since the course of

Abia (Abijah) did not return from Babylon (Ezra 2:36–38). Thus Luke 1:8–9 might have been translated, "And it came to pass, that while he executed the high priest's office before God, in the order of that office according to the law of Moses, which was to burn incense on the altar of incense and wear the breastplate of Aaron containing the sacred lots, before entering the most holy place."

The political implications of a priest (*cohen*) standing up with the Urim and Thummim may have been the underlying motive leading to the arrest and assassination of John the Baptist (Ezra 2:63; Neh. 7:65). When Herod and Rome were in control of Judaea, the high priest's vestments were guarded in the Antonia fortress, because their retention under royal custody was a means of ensuring the docility of the high priest (FF Bruce's *New Testament History*). Yet when Zacharias hid John the Baptist in the wilderness near the Qumran (??Quorum), he could have also stashed there the Urim and Thummim, and John may have revealed them to the Sanhedrin at age 30 in order to inaugurate his ministry. This all would have inflamed the members of the Sanhedrin, yet they would not dare make it public, for they not only knew the political implications, but also that it was the legal right of Zacharias and John the Baptist to do accordingly (Ex. 28:30,43; Num. 20:28; 27:21). It would also explain why in Matthew 21:23–27, the Sanhedrin would not dare question John's authority and Jesus knew it.

In the end, it was the vulpine Herod Antipas, tetrarch of Galilee, who arrested John the Baptist, because

Herod's tetrarchy included the Peraean bank of the Jordan River where much of John's ministry occurred. The Sanhedrin was relieved when it escaped the odium of being directly responsible for his death, for it feared the people, as did Herod (Matt. 14:5; 21:26). In summation, John's arrest and murder may have been more related to the sacred interpreters than to his denouncement of Herod's unlawful marriage and other evils, which may have been revealed only to John via the Urim and Thummim since foxes vitiate their scent (Mark 6; Luke 3:19–20; 13:32).

What about the origin and meaning of the terminology *Urim* and *Thummim?* Scholars believe that the meaning of *Urim* is "lights," but "lights" in Hebrew is *orim.* Where did the *U* come from? The truth is that meanings much deeper than lights and perfections are encrypted in the terms *Urim* and *Thummim.* As an appetizer, it is more than coincidence that the mirror-image of *Urim*, a Hebrew word read from right to left, is *miru* the Japanese verb meaning "to see." (The Japanese are descendants of Japheth, a son of Noah who had the Urim and Thummim and spoke the Adamic language.)

Moreover, the English word *thaumatology* is the study of miracles. Most think *thauma* comes from the Greek, but it really comes from the Hebrew word *thaumah* (תמה) meaning "miracle," and is related to Thummim. (Both have the root תמ meaning *integrity*, and certainly there is a relationship between miracles and integrity.)

Finally, the word *thumb* is also related to Thummim. The *b* in thumb is silent, but in the Hebrew it means "in." Therefore, the miracle in the hand is the thumb, the apposing digit, which distinguishes primates from the rest of the animal world.

But all these are just hors d'oeuvres. Consider for a moment that the *im* (ים) in Urim and Thummim does not signify a plural as much as it does the *im* in Elohim (אלהים), in the same way that the *ah* in Jeremiah, Elijah, Micah, Sarah, Abraham, Methuselah, etc. refers to Jehovah. If so, the terms would mean the light and integrity of Elohim, since אור means *light* and תמ means *integrity*. Comparatively, the word *aura* comes from *orah,* which is Hebrew for the "light of Jehovah," and *thaumah* is Hebrew for "miracle," but it also means the "integrity of Jehovah."

Another example of this etymology is the "Day of Atonement," which in Hebrew is *Yom ha Kippurim* (Lev 23:27; 25:9). Notice that the English translation is not "Day of Atonements." This is a special case where the *im* is not a plural, but from the name *Elohim*. Thus Yom Kippur is really the day of Elohim's Atonement (via Jehovah).

Moreover, in Genesis 1:1, the word *shemayim* is used in the Hebrew and is translated "heaven," not "heavens." *Shem* means "name," not "heaven," so once again, the *im* is not a plural. A better literal translation of *shemayim* would be the "name of Elohim," which is an ideal expression for heaven since God not only created heaven, but also resides and presides there. *In the beginning God created the "name of Elohim" and the earth?*

Yet another example is the word *chaiim* (חיים) which means "life" not "lives." Once again the *im* is not a plural, but from Elohim the giver of life (Gen. 2:7). *Chaiim* is also unique because it has the other members of the Godhead encrypted in it. The *ii* or " is Jehovah and the *chet* (ח) comes from *Ruach* (רוח) or the Holy Ghost.

One final example is the terminology *Kudshah Kudshim* which literally means the "holiness of Jehovah and Elohim" and figuratively the "most holy place" (Ex. 26:34). Once again, the *im* is not a plural and "Holy of Holies" is a misnomer.

Given the above, it is expedient to zoom in and take a closer look at the Hebrew for Urim and Thummim the same way we did earlier with *Borashes*. In the Hebrew, Urim begins with an *aleph* and Thummim begins with a *tau*, and *aleph-tau* is a symbol of Jehovah (see pp. 71–73). Thus Jehovah is cryptogrammatically encoded along with Elohim in the terminology Urim and Thummim.

If one finishes the Hebraic cryptogram, the third member of the Godhead also appears. The *u* (ו) and the *resh* (ר) in Urim come from *Ruach*, the Holy Ghost, and the first *mem* in *Thummim* when added to *ru* makes *rum*. The Hebrew word *rum* (pronounced room) means "to elevate oneself or to be lifted up of the heart," which is a function of the Holy Ghost. Interestingly, the *rum* in the English words *rum*—a spirit, *rheum*—tears, *rumba*—a spiritual dance, *rumble*—the still, small voice, *ruminate*—a function of the Holy Ghost, *rummage*—to search, *quorum*—where one is edified, and *rumor*—Hebrew for the light of the Holy Ghost, all come from the Hebrew word *rum*. It is apparent that we better make *room* for the Holy Ghost in our lives.

In summation, all the members of the Godhead are cryptogrammically found in the terminology Urim and Thummim, just as they are in *Chaiim* (חיים) and *Roshes* (ראשית), and God intended it that way when He coined the words. This is not found in the scriptures because it was either lost through apostasy, or it was not revealed until now because of its sacred nature. Yet it all should now be obvious to the Jews as well as the Latter-day Saints because the words are more acronyms than cryptograms to the Jews.

Let's shift our discussion from the origin and meaning of the terminology Urim and Thummim to their function. Because of the sacred nature of these holy instruments, they were worn in an ornate breastplate, a symbol of righteousness (Eph. 6:14) and faith and love (1 Thes. 5:8), over the heart (Ex. 28:30) where the Lord judges our integrity (1 Sam. 16:7). The instruments would not work unless the user was authorized to use them, and he studied it out in his mind and asked in faith with an honest heart (1 Sam. 28:6; D&C 8;9). Somehow they detect spiritual light and are energized by it. Perhaps this spiritual light is prismatically propagated into *one eternal round* (see glyphic on p. 4).

Joseph Smith did leak clues concerning the sacred instruments and their revelatory functions, just as the high priests and prophets did in the Old Testament and the Book of Mormon. Joseph Smith disclosed that one of the functions of the Urim and Thummim is to know the mysteries of God, which is the *gift of Aaron* (D&C 8:6–8). Moreover, not only are the interpreters guarded by God (Alma 37:16; D&C 8:4), but also they can be used to overcome an enemy, in the same way Eleazar and Phinehas used them to guide and counsel Joshua in his march through the promised land (Num. 27:21; 31:6; Josh.). Imagine if they were used to fight terrorism.

The link between the interpreters and the mysteries of God also includes *one eternal round* (1 Ne. 10:19; Alma 37:11–12). Joseph Smith revealed through the Urim and Thummim that the Lord's *"paths are straight,"* yet *"his course is one eternal round"* (Alma 7:20; 37:12; D&C 3:2). Was he also describing how a Urim and Thummim works? If light passes through a prismatic system as depicted in the glyphic on page 4, it travels in *straight lines* both inside and outside the prisms' media, yet the course of that light is *one eternal round,* which causes the Urim and Thummim to light up until they are disassembled. This would explain why Joseph Smith worked in the dark so that the sacred lots would only detect spiritual light.

Joseph Smith also revealed that the place where God resides is a great Urim and Thummim, and that when the earth is celestialized, it too will be a Urim and Thummim, made like unto crystal. Moreover, those obtaining celestial glory will each be given a Urim and Thummim with a new name on it (D&C 130). Since the New Jerusalem will be cube-shaped (Rev. 21:16), and the *most holy place* is cube-shaped (1 Kgs. 6:20), the Urim and Thummim are probably two diamond-like prisms that can fit together to make a cube.

The Urim and Thummim were also used to issue church callings (1 Chron. 24:5, 31; 25:8; 26:13–14; D&C 14:11), identify sinners (Josh. 7:16–18; 1 Sam. 14:40–42; D&C 10), and determine the distribution of land inheritances, which were divided and arranged *by lot* through the Urim and Thummim (Num. 33:54; 36:3; Josh. 14). The terminology *by lot* originally did not connote a gamble, but rather an allotment from God through the Urim and Thummim. In fact, wherever it says in the English that they *cast lots* (1 Chron. 24:31; 26:13), the word used in the Hebrew for *lots* is *goralot* (גורלות), meaning "little stones." Leviticus 16:8 specifically mentions two lots, one is the Urim and the other is the Thummim. 1 Samuel 14:41 reads "Give a perfect *lot*," but in the marginal rendition, Saul says: "If the guilt be in me or in Jonathan my son, Jahweh, God of Israel, *give Urim*; but if thus thou say: It is in my people Israel; *give Thummim*." Finally, the English word *lot* is a transliteration of the Hebrew לאת meaning "to Jehovah." (Once again, the importance of the *aleph-tau* is illustrated.)

Thus it is clear that originally, the casting of lots involved the Urim and Thummim, but over time through apostasy it degenerated into a satanic gamble such as a *lottery*, or imitation peep stones and crystal balls (D&C 28:11). Moreover, Acts 1:26 states, "And they gave forth their *lots*; and the *lot* fell upon Matthias," who filled the vacancy created by Judas Iscariot's suicide. In this case, The Quorum of the Twelve either used John the Baptist's Urim and Thummim, or an authorized substitute method similar to the one Joseph Smith established (D&C 102:12–34).

The inheritances obtained by allotment through the Urim and Thummim were also lost through unfaithfulness (Ezra 2:62–63; Neh. 7:64–65). Joseph Smith predicted in D&C 85 that the lots of inheritance obtained through the Urim and Thummim and the loss of inheritance as a result of unrighteousness would all happen again someday in the Latter-day Church. The *mighty and strong one* mentioned in verse 7 pertains to one holding the Urim and Thummim of Aaron, and he will probably be the Presiding Bishop of the Church since D&C 58 and 107 indicate that the Presiding Bishop has responsibility over the temporal affairs of the church including land and money. He will also probably be a literal descendant of Aaron since D&C 68 and 107 both say that a literal descendant of Aaron has legal right to the office, provided he is worthy, in the same way Abraham had legal right to the patriarchal birthright based on his worthiness and bloodline (Abr. 1:2).

Other evidence that Joseph Smith was a true prophet is in the recording of the events that transpired when he was ordained with the Aaronic priesthood on May 15, 1829. When John the Baptist appeared, he did not say that he was John the Baptist, but rather he declared: *"I am he who is known as John the Baptist in the New Testament"* (D&C 13). It would be counter-culture for a good Jewish boy to be called John the Baptist; his real name was a good Jewish name: *Yochanaton ben Zachariot ha Cohen,* which in English means "Jonathan, the son of Zacharias, the priest of Aaron." So to make it simple for Joseph Smith and Oliver Cowdery, he did not use his real name. You can imagine John the Baptist using his real name and Joseph Smith pulling a pen out from behind his ear and asking, "Would you mind spelling that, please?" or "Would you please repeat your name for me?"

John the Baptist also said, *"Upon you my fellow servants in the name of Messiah."* If Joseph Smith were a fraud, it would say that John the Baptist appeared to him and conferred the priesthood in the name of Jesus Christ. John the Baptist was not familiar with the terminology *Jesus Christ*, which comes from the Greek, but he knew inside and out the term *Messiah*. Moreover, the *fellow servants* is highly significant since priesthood holders are servants. But they are not slaves since the word slave connotes an absence of freedom, which is contrary to the way the Lord works.

In D&C 13, John the Baptist concludes by saying that the sacrifice to the Lord recorded in Leviticus 9 will be repeated in the future by the *Cohens* with the help of the Levites. It is doubtful that Joseph Smith would have included this if John the Baptist did not say it. Oliver Cowdery's recording of the event, *"that the sons of Levi may yet offer an offering unto the Lord in righteousness,"* connotes that the Aaronic priesthood will never again be taken from the earth. Joseph Smith's version implies that it will be taken from the earth after the sacrifice is offered. It seems that in this aspect, Oliver Cowdery's recollection of the auspicious event is more accurate, because Malachi 3:3 states both in the English and the Hebrew, *"that the sons of Levi may offer unto the Lord an offering in righteousness."* Surely if there are ministering angels in the celestial kingdom, and the Aaronic priesthood holds the keys of these angels, then the Aaronic priesthood is eternal.

It is incredible that John the Baptist, who held the keys of the Aaronic priesthood, did not mention something about the Urim and Thummim of Aaron to Joseph Smith when he restored the Aaronic priesthood. In fact, he probably was wearing the breastplate of Aaron when he appeared on May 15, 1829. Joseph Smith still had the brother of Jared's Urim and Thummim (D&C 17:1), and John the Baptist may have shown him Aaron's Urim and Thummim, given him some tips on how to use a Urim and Thummim, or explained to him that Aaron's Urim and Thummim would be returned to the earth when a worthy literal descendant of Aaron was anointed the Presiding Bishop of the Church. He may have also mentioned something about his book (D&C 93:15,18) which probably discusses these topics. He would have forbidden Joseph Smith to record explicit details concerning such.

Was there a reason why the event occurred on the banks of the Susquehanna River? The name *Susquehanna* actually comes from the Hebrew: *Sus* means "horse," *que* means "to hope" (*Hatikva* is Israel's national anthem and means "the future hope"), and *hannah* means "grace of Jehovah." The priesthood is God's workhorse, it renders hope, and was received by the grace of Jehovah.

There is more overlap between Judaism and what Joseph Smith revealed about the Aaronic priesthood versus the Levitical order. The first mention of ordinations **other than** Aaron and his sons, who were priests, is Numbers 3:6. (The ordinations of Aaron and his sons occurred in Ex. 28.) Even the entire book of Leviticus only discusses sacerdotal functions of Aaron and his sons, and so its name is a **misnomer** and should be *Aaronicus*. This is corroborated by the book's title ויקרא in the Hebrew Bible, which title means *"And the Lord Called."* When the priest *manqué* Korah, who was born a Levite, rebelled against Moses, he flouted Aaron's authority by trumpeting that he was a fungible and should be defrocked. It is clear from Moses' retort, *"Seek ye the priesthood also?"* that there is a distinct difference between the Aaronic and Levitical priesthoods (Num. 16:9–10). In the very next chapter, in order to prove Aaron's legal right to the priesthood, God has Moses place a rod from each tribe of Israel in the tabernacle. The names of each prince representing the twelve tribes were inscribed on their respective rods, and Aaron's name was on the rod of Levi. The next day, Aaron's rod was the only one budding, blooming, and yielding almonds. This substantiated Aaron's legal right to the keys of the Aaronic priesthood, and his rod was placed in the Ark of the Covenant as a permanent memento of this.

As an interesting aside, there is something special about almonds since Aaron's rod yielded them, Jacob sent almonds to Joseph in Egypt (Gen. 43:11), the candlestick in the tabernacle had four bowls shaped like almonds (Ex. 37:20), Jeremiah when he was called was shown a rod of an almond tree (Jer. 1:11), and Solomon admired the almond tree (Ecc. 12:5). The almond tree is the first to arouse and awake after the sleep of winter, and the Hebrew word for almond is שָׁקֵד which also means to watch, even to the point of sleeplessness. Therefore, the almond is a symbol of ardour, vigilance, and the priesthood, and priesthood holders are to be valiant in their faith, and vigilantly watch, not only for the Lord (Matt. 24:42), but also over the flock. Could there also be significance in the similarity between the words *almond, alms,* and *Alma* (virgin in Hebrew; soul in Spanish; beneficent in Latin)?

D&C 107:1 also countenances a distinction between the Aaronic and Levitical priesthoods; it states that **the Aaronic includes the Levitical.** (It should also say this in D&C 107:6 instead of *Aaronic or Levitical,* and in Hebrews 7:11, it should say, "If therefore perfection were by the Aaronic priesthood which includes the Levitical.") D&C 107:85–88 says that the bishop is the president of the priests but not of the deacons and teachers, and calls him the *president over the priesthood of Aaron.* (Consequently, D&C 107:10 should say "priest of the Aaronic order" instead of *priest of the Levitical order.*) Sections 68:15–21 and 107:16 speak specifically of *literal descendants of Aaron.* Even the Lord distinguished between the two in his parable of the Good Samaritan: in the parable, first a *priest* came along, and then a *Levite* followed. Jesus would not have used the terms *priest* and *Levite* if they were synonymous: it would be a redundancy. Kings David and Solomon also knew there was a distinction between the two as the terminology *the priests and the Levites* were also used in their day (1 Chron. 23:27–28; 2 Chron. 5:5; 11:13–14).

The taxonomy that exists with Jewish names also supports that there is a distinction between the Aaronic and Levitical orders. כהן is pronounced *cohen,* and is Hebrew for "priest of the Aaronic order, a literal descendant of Aaron," while the Hebrew word for "false priest" is *cumor* (2 Kgs. 23:5). Since the meaning of a word in Hebrew is derived only from the consonants and not the vowels (with the exception of the tokens of the Godhead—see chapter 11), there are other names that comply with the phonetic sounds of the consonants *c, h,* and *n* from the word *cohen.* For example, Kahn and Cohn. The Levitical order is represented by names such as Levy, Levitt, Levinson, Lewis, and Levine. The Jews also make a distinction on high holy days *Rosh Hashanah* and *Yom Kippur*

(New Year's Day and Day of Atonement). During the services on those days, the Rabbi will bark out *Cohanim* and the literal descendants of Aaron will go to a specified area where there is a sink with running water and clean towels. The Levites will meet the *Cohens* there and remove the *Cohens'* shoes and then proceed to wash the hands of the *Cohens* three times a certain way (Ex. 30:19–21). Then, after the Levites dry the hands of the *Cohens*, the *Cohens* march up to the pulpit area in their stocking feet, place their silk shawls called *talasim* over their heads to cover their faces, and say in Hebrew the special prayer of the *Cohens* (Num. 6:24–26).

A distinction between the two priesthoods can also be derived from the Ark of the Covenant. The Hebrew word for "Ark of the Covenant" is *ahron* (ארון) which is very similar to *Aaron* (אהרן). Moreover, the responsibility and privilege to care for the Ark, cover it, carry it into battle, and use it to part the river Jordan belonged to Aaron and his literal descendants, the *Cohens* (Num. 4:5–15; Josh. 3:6,13; 4:9–10; 6:6).

A distinction can also be made with the tabernacle, which is *mishcon* (משכן) in Hebrew: mish (מש) comes from Moses (משה) and con (כן) comes from *cohen* (כהן) meaning "priest of Aaron."

D&C 20:58,64 also makes a distinction between the two priesthoods by stating that priests can ordain other priests, teachers, and deacons, baptize, administer the sacrament, or lay on hands, but teachers and deacons cannot perform these functions just as the Levitical order in Judaism was limited as compared to the Aaronic priesthood authority.

Shortly after receiving the Aaronic priesthood, Joseph Smith received the Melchizedek priesthood at the hands of Peter, James, and John. Melchizedek is only mentioned in Genesis chapter 14 of the Hebrew Bible and so the Jews know little about him, but Joseph Smith revealed clues about Melchizedek's identity. In D&C 84:14 it states that Melchizedek received the priesthood through the lineage of his **fathers**, even till Noah. If Shem were Melchizedek, it would say father, not fathers. Abraham 1:5 states, *"My fathers, having turned from their righteousness."* At least Abraham's father Terah and grandfather Nehor were unrighteous, so neither are Melchizedek because, among other things, *melchizedek* is Hebrew for "king of righteousness." Since the Hebrews are descendants of Eber (this is corroborated in McConkie's *Mormon Doctrine)*, and Melchizedek is mentioned more times in the book of Hebrews than any other book in the Bible, it fits that Eber is Melchizedek.

Joseph Smith also restored the *laying on of hands* in order to ordain someone. Examples of this procedure in the stick of Judah include Jacob bestowing the birthright on Ephraim (Gen. 48:14), and Moses conferring the keys of the Kingdom on Joshua (Num. 27:18). Ironically, it is not practiced in Judaism today, even though it is countenanced in the Torah. Also an enigma to the Jews is the Melchizedek priesthood which requires the *laying on of hands.*

Chapter 9
Elias(h), Elijah, and Temple Ordinances

The link between Elias and Elijah not only includes their mutual appearances on April 3, 1836 (D&C 110), but also their names sometimes are used interchangeably: *Elias* is Greek for "Elijah" and "Elias." For instance, there are 18 references to Elias in the New Testament and only four do not pertain to Elijah. But knowing this does not eliminate the obfuscation about Elias. Both the Bible dictionary and McConkie's *Mormon Doctrine* give several definitions or applications of Elias based on what Joseph Smith revealed on the subject. Yet here is another example where Joseph Smith's sketch was incomplete or adumbrated. This is evident by merely looking at the Joseph Smith Translation of Mark 9:3 where Joseph notions that the Elias mentioned in Mark 9:4 is John the Baptist. However, John the Baptist could not have been embodied on the Mount of Transfiguration because he was dead (Mark 6), and had not been resurrected yet since Jesus had yet to be resurrected and Jesus was the first fruits of the resurrection. All of the heavenly visitors on the Mount of Transfiguration had to have translated bodies because keys were bestowed by the *laying on of hands*. Nevertheless, Joseph Smith deserves a lot of credit because he knew there is a distinction between Elijah and Elias, and he revealed most of the doctrine of Elias which was lost as there is no mention of Elias in the Old Testament.

The key to a complete understanding of the doctrine of Elias is in the Hebrew (as well as the Greek), which Joseph Smith had not mastered. When the angel Gabriel (Luke 1), John the Baptist (JST John 1) and the Lord (Matt. 11:14; 17:12; Mark 9:12) used the title, they did not say the English or Greek *Elias,* but the Hebrew ***Eliash,*** which means **"my God is fire."** (In Luke 1:17, Gabriel said *Eliash,* not *Eliyahu* (Elijah), even though some Malachi phraseology is used.) When Elijah was the subject of conversation with the Jews, they said *Eliyahu* (my God is Jehovah), not the English *Elijah* or the Greek *Elias.*

During John the Baptist's ministry, Jewish leaders thought he might be Elijah because of what Malachi prophesied about Elijah's return. When they inquired it of him, John the Baptist figured it was a good teaching opportunity so he answered in Hebrew that he was neither *Eliyahu* (Elijah) nor the Messiah, but *Eliash* (JST John 1:21). Yet the Jews pressed him further asking, "How then art thou *Eliash?*" He went on to explain that he was not that "God of fire" who was to follow him and "*baptize...with fire, and with the Holy Ghost*" (JST John 1:28). Then they grasped how he was *Eliash*—**he was not spiritual fire, his God was.**

It follows that anyone who is a forerunner of God's fire is an Elias(h), John the Baptist being the perfect example. Noah (Gabriel) was the first Elias(h)

(D&C 27:6–7) because he oversaw the baptism of the earth with water in preparation for its baptism by fire. Thus he was given the privilege of annunciation (Luke 1:11–20). John the Revelator is also an Elias(h) because he is preparing the earth for the great and dreadful day of the Lord that will burn as an oven (D&C 77:14; Mal. 4).

The interchangeability of the *s* and *sh* in Elias(h) is related to the effect of transliteration and dialect on translation. There is no *sh* in Greek so naturally the Greeks transliterated *Eliash* as *Elias*. Moreover the Hebrew letter ש is either a *shin* or a *sin*: the word *shibboleth* was pronounced *sibboleth* by the Ephraimites (Judg. 12:5–6). Another example of this could be the name *S(h)inai* (see p. 68).

The auspicious appearances on April 3, 1836 in the Kirtland Temple (D&C 110) paralleled those on the Mount of Transfiguration and are clues as to what really happened on the mount. There are 18 references to Elias in the New Testament. Matthew 11:14; 17:12; Mark 9:13; and Luke 1:17 refer to Elias(h). Matthew 16:14; 27:47; Mark 6:15; 8:28; 15:35; Luke 9:8, 19, 54; John 1:21; Romans 11:2; and James 5:17 are all in reference to Elijah. Notice that Matthew, Mark, and Luke all use the name *Elias* for either Elias(h) or Elijah. The remaining three references on Elias pertain to the Mount of Transfiguration (Matt. 17:3; Mark 9:4; Luke 9:30). Elders Talmage and McConkie say that this Elias refers to Elijah; **but the original Greek probably indicated *Elias* and *Elias*.** When it was translated into the English or rewritten in Greek, the translators and scribes thought it was a redundancy, so they wrote just *Elias*. **Thus here it refers to both Elijah and Elias(h).** The three tabernacles that Peter offered to make were for Moses, Elijah, and Elias so they would not leave. When the Greeks and the English dropped the second Elias, they assigned the third tabernacle to the Lord.

It never dawned on Joseph Smith that there were three heavenly visitors with bodies on the Mount of Transfiguration. But in a way, this is evidence that his visitations were real because they correlate perfectly with the Mount of Transfiguration and he did not even realize it.

Who was the Elias on the Mount of Transfiguration and in the Kirtland Temple on Passover, 1836 that committed the dispensation of the gospel of Abraham (D&C 110:12)? McConkie states in *Mormon Doctrine* under the subtitle "Elias" that he was a contemporary of Abraham of unknown identity. But then under the subtitle "Gabriel," Elder McConkie intimates that he is Noah who "*conferred the keys of his dispensation upon Joseph Smith.*" This is erroneous since Joseph Smith received the keys of Abraham's dispensation from Elias. Although the authors admit that the Elias who appeared to Joseph Smith could have been Noah, they prefer Melchizedek for the following reasons:

1. Melchizedek was more of a contemporary to Abraham than Noah. Noah may have raised Abraham (book of Jasher), but Melchizedek

ordained him to the patriarchal order (Heb. 7:1–7; JST Gen. 14:25–40; D&C 84:14).

2. Melchizedek was more likely than Noah to have been translated, and translation was crucial for those who appeared on the Mount of Transfiguration because keys were bestowed by *the laying on of hands.* Consequently, Satan threw a tantrum when Moses was translated (Jude 1:9), and probably had a similar fit when Elijah was translated. There is no intimation anywhere in the scriptures of Noah being translated. In fact Genesis 9:29 states that he died. Contradistinctively, Hebrews 7:3 says that Melchizedek had not end of life. Moreover, the Joseph Smith Translation of Genesis 14:27 states: *"he was ordained an high priest after the order of the covenant which God made with Enoch,"* the seventh patriarch. This order has power to control the physical elements and be translated (JST Gen. 14:30–32). It continues by saying that Melchizedek (Eber), the 14th patriarch, was called the king of heaven and sought for the City of Enoch which was translated (JST Gen. 14:34–36). Since God's house is a house of order, it is a perfect fit that the 14th patriarch would be translated just like the seventh. Noah did not need a body for the annunciation since there were no keys bestowed.

3. Although Noah is an Elias(h), a forerunner of God's fire, so is Melchizedek. Five times in the "book" of Hebrews the Lord is called *"a high*

115

priest forever after the order of Melchizedek" (5:6, 10; 6:20; 7:17, 21), and the Joseph Smith Translation of Genesis 14:35 says *"that the sons of God should be tried so as by fire."*

4. Melchizedek did not have a dispensation while Noah had his own, separate from Abraham's. Melchizedek, not Abraham, was given the privilege of committing Abraham's dispensation because although Abraham directly received the promises, Melchizedek was greater than Abraham (Heb. 7:7; Alma 13:19), was probably translated, and was a forerunner of the dispensation. Evidence that Melchizedek indeed did prepare for Abraham's dispensation is that Abraham was a Hebrew, a descendant of Eber, yet anyone who was a Hebrew in spirit and belief was also a Hebrew and had Melchizedek (Eber) as his or her spiritual progenitor. This is why Paul calls himself *"an Hebrew of the Hebrews"* (Philip. 3:5). Melchizedek started the spiritual adoption process (see gospel of Abraham below).

5. Peter, James, and John restored the Melchizedek priesthood because they were the last to hold the keys of that priesthood, but they probably received those keys from Melchizedek on the Mount of Transfiguration.

6. Every time the authors ponder and pray on the matter, they get a stupor of thought when they propose Noah to be this Elias.

What exactly is the gospel of Abraham? According to McConkie in *Mormon Doctrine*, the gospel of

Abraham is synonymous with celestial marriage, but it actually is much more than that. Not only does it include the law of circumcision and the branding of Jehovah into Abraham and Sarah (see pp. 129–130), but according to Galatians chapter 3, the gospel of Abraham is the promise that all of the faithful are the seed of Abraham whether by pure descent or by adoption. In fact the last verse states, *"If ye be Christ's, then are ye Abraham's seed, and heirs"* (see also Mosiah 14:8; 15:10–11). It is through the gospel of Abraham that now there is so much adoption into the house of Israel through patriarchal blessings, which are not a declaration of lineage (except in the cases of literal descendants of Aaron and the patriarchal birthright bloodline), but rather a declaration of the inherited blessings of that lineage (Eldred G. Smith).

It was during the dispensation of the gospel of Abraham that the patriarchal order came to an end. (Ephraim was the last patriarch of this order.) The patriarchal order consisted of a government where the patriarch wore two hats, one for the patriarchal birthright, the other as the prophet holding the keys of the kingdom. A new order arose in the house of Israel where the hats were separated so that the prophet who held the keys of the Kingdom did not need the patriarchal bloodline birthright. (Notice that by the time Moses came on the scene, he was able to hold the keys of the Kingdom without having the patriarchal birthright.) It was through the dispensation of the gospel of Abraham that this transition took place. There were so many more spirits that needed the blessings of the patriarchal order but would not obtain them with that order, that the Lord changed the system. For example, God commanded Abram to marry Hagar and they had a son, but Abram knew that Ishmael would not get the birthright. This grieved Abram because he loved Ishmael, but with the new order of adoption into the house of Israel on the horizon, Ishmael and his descendants could get the same blessings as Isaac if they were righteous and accepted Jesus Christ as their Savior.

There is also much overlap between Judaism and what Joseph Smith revealed about Elijah. He is called the *Tishbite*, but 1 Kings 17:1 says he is from *Gilead,* which is east of the Jordan river, and *Tishbah* is a town in Naphtali, west of the Jordan. Is Elijah the Tishbite because he held the keys of the temple ordinances and he prophesied that the Temple would be destroyed on *Tisha Bov?*

The Jews have a special place setting of silverware, cup, and napkin for Elijah, along with a special chair for him to sit on during the lavish Passover feast called the *Seder.* During the Seder service, the door to the house is opened so that Elijah the prophet is invited into the home. This is so the curse mentioned in Malachi will not come upon that household and the people in attendance. The Jews even joke about this opening of the door for Elijah. If someone hears a knock at the door and opens it and nobody is there, then the person opening the door will say, *"It must have been Elijah."* During the Passover Seder, a young person, usually a boy of bar mitzvah age (13) is requested to ask the four questions and sit to the left of the patriarch; Elijah's chair is to the right. The Jews to this day are fatuously clinging to the sterile belief that Elijah, as well as the Messiah, have not yet come and are still waiting for them. But Elijah has already come when he visited Joseph Smith and Oliver Cowdery in the Kirtland Temple on **Passover**, 1836 (D&C 110).

It is also interesting that the last part of the Hebrew Bible mentions Elijah, and the first scripture out of Moroni's mouth when he appeared to Joseph Smith was the end of Malachi with a twist: *"And he shall plant in the hearts of the children the promises made to the fathers, and the hearts of the children shall turn to their fathers. If it were not so, the whole earth would be utterly wasted at his coming."* When Elijah came on April 3, 1836, he quoted Malachi verbatim rather than using Moroni's version. Both renditions of Malachi are applicable.

Joseph Smith taught through the temple endowment, which was probably approved by Elijah when he came, that in order to make it to the Celestial Kingdom, one has to be able to live the law of consecration. The word *consecrate* in the Hebrew is מלאיד which literally means "fill the hand." When studying the story of Gideon, the Lord had him reduce his army of 32,000 men to 300 lest Israel vaunt themselves (Judg. 7:2). First he dismissed the fearful, those 22,000 who lacked faith, then he took the remaining 10,000 to a water hole and only those who drank from a cupped hand were retained. The Lord was probably giving a lesson on consecration, for the "cupped hand" is an important part of temple worship including the superannuated thurification.

Elijah also held the keys of initiatory work in the temple where saints are anointed to become kings and priests, and queens and priestesses. The unction is very similar to the one David received from Samuel when he was anointed king.

The Hebrew Bible has examples of righteous people receiving a new name. For example, Abram was changed to Abraham, Sarai to Sarah, Jacob to Israel, Hoshea to Joshua, and Naomi to Marah. New names were also given in the New Testament: Simon to Peter, John to Mark, Saul to Paul, and so on. Isaiah also taught that a new and improved name would be given to the righteous, and it would be everlasting (Isaiah 56:5). Joseph Smith revealed that a new name should be given in the endowment ordinance.

The Jewish Bible also mentions the veil in the tabernacle and the temple (Ex. 26:31–33; 2 Chron. 3:14). There is also a veil in Mormon temples. Furthermore, Isaiah 22:23–25 mentions the *nail in the sure place,* and Isaiah 24:5 mentions the *everlasting covenant.* Both are an important part of the Mormon temple ceremony. Lastly, *yad le El* is "hand to God," "foot to God" would be *regel le El*, and *pe le El* means "mouth to God." This is one of the reasons why Joseph Smith studied Hebrew in the School of the Prophets.

It is likely that Elijah also revealed to Joseph Smith that the tokens of the Aaronic and Melchizedek priesthoods together are a cryptogram. The message of the cryptogram is *Jesus Christ who was crucified is the Holy (Almighty) One of Israel.*

One of the tokens of the Melchizedek priesthood also will be used in the ordinance of the resurrection (Isaiah 56:5; Mark 5:41). In Isaiah 56:5, the Hebrew not only mentions a new name, but also the word *yad* (hand) and the obscure and arcane word *bechomosaiy* (בחומתי), which probably is the Hebrew word for "resurrection." The ב means *in*, the ח stands for *life*, the ו stands for *create*, and the מתי means *my death.* Therefore the word means *"in life created by my death"* which is the resurrection, and Jesus is the first fruits of the resurrection. The word *yad* is used for three reasons: One, since it holds the scepter, it represents the power of God or the priesthood. Two, *yad* was originally *yod* (Gesenius' *Hebrew-Chaldee Lexicon to the Old Testament,* p. 325), which is a token of Jehovah. Three, it is used in a special grip when performing the ordinance of the resurrection (Mark 5:41— although revivification is not exactly resurrection, they are fraternal twins, and the special grip is not mentioned because it is sacred). The reason all this does not appear in the English is because the Jews do not believe in a resurrection, nor do they know the Hebrew word for it coined by Isaiah. Moreover, they along with the rest of Christendom do not believe God has a body, and do not know that a special grip of the hand is required for the ordinance of the resurrection. (This is another prime example of a mistranslation in the Bible, and Isaiah 56 was not on the Gold Plates that Joseph Smith translated.)

Not only do mistranslations arise over time, but also fairy tales and fantasies. When the Lord raised Jairus' daughter from the dead (Mark 5:41), He used the word *cumi,* meaning "arise." After Jesus performed the miracle, it was rumored that the Lord used a magic potion called *alchemy* to perform it. *Al* means "God," and "chemy" comes from *cumi.* Since then, *alchemy* has been used to mean the "elixir of life." Milton wrote, *"Four speedy cherubim put to their mouths the sounding alchemy."* Why would Milton write *sounding alchemy* if he were not referring to what the Lord spoke (*cumi*) when He brought back to life Jairus' daughter? Also, Shakespeare wrote, *"Guilding pale streams with heavenly alchemy."* Why would Shakespeare describe alchemy as heavenly if the *al* did not refer to God?

Although Elijah had the keys for temple ordinances, he did not have keys for the ordinances of resurrection and creation. Only the Lord holds those keys.

It is also within the purview of this chapter to touch on solemn assemblies. In Deuteronomy 9:10, Moses refers to the auspicious event of Moses, Aaron, Nadab, Abihu, and 70 elders of Israel seeing Elohim as *the assembly,* and it was obviously a solemn one if Elohim and Jehovah were present. This implies that at least one member of the Godhead is present at a solemn assembly, and ideally, those in attendance should see Him, or at least feel His presence (Ex. 13:21–22; 40:34; 1 Kgs. 8:10–12).

Chapter 10
Other Insights from Judaism

There are other precious insights to be gained from Judaism. According to the law of Moses, Levites could not start their ministry until age 30 (Num. 4). Thus, the reason why Jesus waited until age 30 to be baptized is that John the Baptist could not baptize Him until John the Baptist was thirty, and He was only six months younger than John the Baptist (Luke 1).

The law of Moses also states that Passover is a seven-day holiday, and the first and the seventh days of the Passover are Sabbath days (Ex. 12:16; Lev. 23:7). The scriptures teach us that Jesus was crucified on Passover, but before the Sabbath (John 19:31). The Sabbath referred to could have been the last day of Passover (which may have fallen on a Thursday), rather than the hebdomadal Saturday Sabbath. This would explain Ash Wednesday, if Jesus were crucified on the Wednesday before the Passover Sabbath. A Wednesday crucifixion would also signify that Jesus was in the tomb three days and three nights since he resurrected after sundown Saturday, which is the start of the first day of the week (Sunday) by Jewish reckoning. This would satisfy His own teaching that He would be in the belly of the earth three days and three nights (Matt. 12:40). It would also be in harmony with what was revealed in the stick of Joseph—namely, that He would rise **after** three days (2 Ne. 25:13; Hel. 14:20). Thus the hebdomadal Sabbath was changed from the seventh day (Saturday) to the first day (Sunday) to commemorate the greatest event (the resurrection) since the creation of the earth (Acts 20:7).

There are other confusions on the calendar. Passover starts on the 14th day of the first month and ends on the 21st day of the first month (Ex. 12; Lev. 23:5). The reason why the Lord, Moses, Elias, and Elijah all chose to come on April 3, 1836 (D&C 110) and not any other day is to show the Jews who wait for Elijah on Passover that the first day of Passover is April 3rd, which puts *Rosh Hashanah* (New Year's Day) on the vernal equinox. Yet the world celebrates New Year's Day on Jan 1st, and the Jews celebrate *Rosh Hashanah* near the autumnal equinox.

Christmas is another twisted religious holiday. It commemorates the Lord's birth, yet the Lord's birthday is not December 25th, but April 6th (D&C 20:1). Moreover, Satan loves the fact that Santa, a dyslexic form of Satan, gets more attention than the Lord. (Another example of satanic twisting is Zion and Nazi.)

Easter is worse. The word *Easter* appears only once in all of the LDS scriptures as a mistranslation of the Greek word *paskha* for Passover (Acts 12:3–4), and comes from Ashtoreth, the Philistine goddess of love and fertility (1 Sam. 31:10). The plural of Ashtoreth is

Ashteroth. If the *oth*, the Hebrew female plural suffix is dropped, the remaining word is *Ashter* or Easter. (The Bible dictionary does not go back far enough, for it says that Easter comes from a Norse goddess.) Ashtoreth and Baal were the false gods that corrupted the Israelites after they entered the promised land (Judg. 2:13; 10:6), and the prophets of the Lord were constantly fighting against them (1 Sam. 7:3–4; 12:10; 1 Kgs. 18). In fact, whoredoms were committed by the Israelites in "love groves" made to Ashtoreth (1 Kgs. 14:15; 16:33). Why would we use a dirty, filthy name for the holiday that celebrates the Lord's resurrection, and why would the Easter bunny get more attention than the Lord? Once again, it is because of Satan's chicanery. What should happen before the Second Coming in preparation for it is that Passover should start on April 3rd, Christmas should fall on April 6th, and Easter should be celebrated on the second Sunday in April and be called *Yom Bechomosai* or the "Resurrection Day" (see p. 121).

Hanukkah is a Jewish holiday commemorating the purification and rededication of the Temple at Jerusalem in 165 B.C. by Judas Maccabeus. At the rededication, the menorah only had oil for a few hours, but miraculously, it lasted eight days. Thus Hanukkah is an eight-day holiday with an eight-candle *menorah*, which is Hebrew for "from the light of Jehovah." Incidentally, the surname *Maccabee* is actually a Hebrew acronym. The *Maccabees* were priests (*cohens*) in Judea approximately a century before Zacharias, the father of John the Baptist, and their name comes from them carrying the words of Exodus 15:11, *"Who is like to thee among the strong, O Lord,"* in which the initial letters in the Hebrew are *M.C.B.E.I.* (מ, ח, ב, ה, י). This is substantiated in 1 Maccabees of the Catholic Bible (Douay Version).

Religious Jews have a ritual called the *mikva*. It is a purification with water. Jewish teenage boys have a joke with a double *entendre* wishing they were life-guards at a mikva. After a Jewish woman delivers a baby and there is an issue of blood, to become clean she must go to the mikva and bathe to wash away the unclean blood. The leper also had to wash with water to become clean (Lev. 13; 14), as did Aaron and his sons who were the priests (Exod. 29:4; Num. 19:7). Isaiah 1:16 also states, *"Wash you, make you clean."* The ablution rituals of the Jews under the leadership and authority of the *Cohens* still exist today and are related to the ordinance of *baptism*, which in the Greek means "an immersion in water." The word *baptize* is not found in the Old Testament because it is a Greek word; the Hebrew word for "baptize" is *taval* (2 Kgs. 5:14). When Jesus came to John to be baptized, He did not say "baptize" me, but "*taval*" me.

The Jews really do not believe in a resurrection and they fear death. Their approach to life is one of *carpe diem*, and they say over and over, *"Eat, drink and be merry, for tomorrow we die."* Their funerals are lugubrious, and they give a prayer in memory of the deceased in the synagogue called the *Yizkor*, meaning "He shall be remembered," which does not connote a life after death.

[handwritten annotations: "awww, Gary"; "How Sad!"; "I wish I would have said more to him!"]

The Jews also believe that the Messiah will come in power to cleanse the earth of wicked people, as did God at the time of Noah, but he will not be a theomaniac, which is considered blasphemy. They do not realize that the Messiah will cleanse the earth by fire at His second coming, but at His first coming was the consummate immolation to atone for our sins. If there is one scripture that gives the characteristics of His first coming more than any other, it is Isaiah the 53rd chapter. What really makes it obvious is when "we the Jews" is read wherever it says *"we,"* and "He the Messiah" wherever it says *"he."* It is such an important chapter that it is quoted in the stick of Joseph (Mosiah 14). Actually, there are 283 direct citations of the Old Testament in the New Testament, 116 coming from the Psalms, substantiating either directly or indirectly that Jesus is the Messiah (Bible Dictionary). Thus the Incarnation was for the Jews something that was predicted.

The law of Moses states in Deut. 6:9 that *"thou shalt write them upon the posts of thy house, and on thy gates."* Consequently, Jews have a *mezuzah* rolled up in a scroll in a case at the entrance to their homes as a reminder of faith in Jehovah. (Tevya in "Fiddler on the Roof" kisses the mezuzah every time he leaves or enters his house in order to demonstrate his faith in Jehovah.) On one side of the parchment is Deut 6:4–9 and 11:13–21, and on the other is the letter *shin*, which is the first letter of the word *shaddai*, which means "almighty."

Jude was the brother of the Lord and he may have been sententious, given his book of only 25 verses, but when you read them it is readily apparent that he was a Torah scholar. He not only mentions in verse nine Satan's temper-tantrum when Moses was translated, because he did not want Moses to have a body for his début on the Mount of Transfiguration. But also in verse 11, he denounces the way of Cain, the doctrine of Balaam, and the gainsaying of Korah, all events that transpired in the Torah. Moses 5:51 states that Cain perpetrated secret combinations that included as part of their codes the homosexual relations between fellow conspirators. The doctrine of Balaam was with avaricious intent, to destroy the saints by corrupting them. Korah aspired for higher callings showing that status-anxiety is evil and that there is a difference between the Aaronic and Levitical priesthoods.

The holiday of *Yom Kippur* (Day of Atonement) is the most holy holiday of Judaism. The religious believe that on Yom Kippur, God writes in his Book of Life those people on earth who will live or die. David Cohen, the authors' father/grandfather, would act as Rabbi on Yom Kippur and *Rosh Hashanah* (New Year's Day), which usually fall in September. In the synagogue, the Jews recite a long prayer called the *al chet,* which means "we have sinned," and each time the *al chet* is repeated (about 35 times), the Jews hit the area over their hearts with a clenched fist. David Cohen would repeatedly beat himself so hard while he was leading the congregation that his son Irving, one of the authors, marveled how he could remain standing.

The law of Moses calls for a day of fasting to afflict one's soul (Lev. 16:29; Num. 29:7) only on Yom Kippur. But religious Jews also fast on *Tisha Bov* which is the day both temples were destroyed, but this fast day came after the law of Moses was given. (Thus, Jews fast only two days a year and Mormons fast at least 12.) Interestingly, there is no kneeling even on this most holy of days, but rather genuflection. Jews never kneel in humility before God, surely an indication of a stiff-necked and hard-hearted people. It is no wonder that Isaiah proclaims that every knee shall bow (Isaiah 45:23; Mosiah 27:31). Since knees usually bend easier than the mind, imagine what it is going to take to get the Jews to change their thinking. Zechariah prophesied that it would take an appearance of the Messiah to the Jews where He actually shows them the wounds in His hands, and then shall there be tremendous guilt and shame, which will cause the Jews to ululate *"as one mourneth for his only son"* (Zech. 12:10; 13:6).

David Cohen the rabbi also preached a sermon in the synagogue on Genesis 17 where the two "h"s are inserted into Abraham and Sarah. He would do so with great emotion and many tears would madefy the pulpit, because an angel had told him that someday he would be given the reason why the "h"s were inserted. Irving, a Jewish convert to the Church, thought he might be the instrument in converting his parents if he discovered the reason, and so he fasted and prayed and the Lord revealed it to him. Because Abram and Sarai would not withhold their only begotten son, God took the two "h"s in Jehovah (יהוה) and branded the first one into

Abram to make Abraham and the second one into Sarai to make Sarah. This was done to show the world that His Only Begotten would descend from Abraham and Sarah through Isaac, their only son. The Spirit continued to reveal that the symbol of that covenant was circumcision, where the father of an innocent boy has to stand and watch his son be inflicted with pain and suffering and his blood spilled as a similitude of the sacrifice of the Messiah. After the crucifixion, the law of circumcision was done away (Moro. 8:8).

When Irving explained all this to his Papa in Yiddish, he was in awe and felt that Irving proved worthy of the birthright of Aaron. He proceeded to give it to Irving, who in turn gave his son the other author, the birthright of Aaron. David was shown by his father in Russia the genealogy in Hebrew documenting that he was indeed a first-born literal descendant of Aaron. This was later confirmed through divine revelation by Irving's patriarchal blessing. Irving's son David was declared by patriarchal blessing to be of the tribe of Ephraim through his mother who is a relative of Ezra Taft Benson, but David would also automatically be a literal descendant of Aaron because of Irving. There may be even more hybridity considering that David has two siblings from the tribe of Judah.

When Irving was bestowed the birthright, he took courage to inform his father that Jesus was the Messiah. As the saying goes, *fools rush in where angels fear to tread.* David took umbrage and was furious and threatened to withdraw the birthright. He called his son a traitor to Judaism among other things and compared him to Eli's sons. But Irving reminded him that when Isaac gave Jacob the birthright thinking he was Esau, he could not revoke the blessing. Needless to say, David did not join the Church because he did not believe Jesus was the Messiah, and gave his disavowed son many harangues on the subject of his conversion. But after he died in 1974, his work for the dead was performed in 1975 by the two authors at the Washington D.C. Temple.

In summation, there are some fascinating parallels between Judaism and Mormonism that dispel any doubt that Joseph Smith was a luminary, and that he restored the true gospel of Jesus Christ. There is no way Joseph Smith could have fraudulently satisfied all of the overlaps illustrated. Moreover, his occasional error or peccadillo lends even greater credibility to his ministry because of his prodigious accomplishments despite being human. His achievements are even more Herculean given he died at age 38 and was constantly on the run from persecution. It is high time the Jews, who were first and are now last, accept Jesus as their Messiah so that the last become first. Mormonism is no ersatz religion!

And now, given that the language of the millennium will be the Adamic (Zeph. 3:9), and that "the alphabet is the miracle of miracles, the greatest of all inventions, by which even the television and jet-planes pale in comparison" (Hugh Nibley's *Temple and Cosmos*, p. 458), to follow is the reward for enduring thus far: a revolutionary view of the original Hebrew or the Adamic language. Enjoy! But first a Jewish song:

Spiritual Vision

A Yiddish Song
Eli, Eli

Religioso

E-li E- - li____ lo ma a - zav-to-ni____ E-li

E - - - - li____ la ma a - zav-to-ni____ In fei-er in

flam hot man uns ge- bre - end und uns ib -er al ge- macht zu sch-and und

shpott doch ob zu ven-den Hot uns kein - er nit ge-kent Fon dir mein

Gott mit dein Heil-i-gen Toir-e und mit dein ge bott. E-li E - Li

Lo-mo-a-sav-to -ni E-li E - li Lo - ro-a- sev - to - ni Tog und na-acht

nor ich tr-ae-cht fur mein Ich beit mit moi-re up dein toir-e dein ge-bott

Re-te nich re-te-nich fon ge-far vie a-mul die u-ves fon-bei esen-gzar

Her mein ge-beit nein ge-vein Hel- fen kanst du nor du a- lein

shma yis-ru- el ad-o-noi e-lo he nu a-do noi e-chod_____

(Mathew 27:46; Psalms 22:1)

132

Chapter 11
Vowels of the Godhead

Biblical Hebrew scholars today believe that there were no vowels in the original Hebrew, and that all 22 letters of the alphabet are consonants (Mansoor's *Biblical Hebrew*, vol. 1:13, 15, 31). Intuitively, this view explains why Hebrew became a dead language, because a language without vowels is dead: vowels are the most important letters of the alphabet since they are speech sounds without any closure or narrowing. When Hebrew was revivified, vowel signs were invented by Jewish Grammarians to resolve the problem of no vowels. In fact, Monsoor states: "Our present vowel system was probably adopted during the ninth or tenth century A.D."—The Dark Ages! Alas, the reality is that the current system is manmade, and thus has limitations and errors. If Mormon confessed that the Nephites altered the Hebrew (Morm. 9:33), imagine what the world has done to it.

The word *vowel* comes from the old French word *vouel* and the word *vow* comes from the French word *vou*. These two words are transliterations of the Hebrew cryptograms בוואל and בוו, which should be solvable to the reader via chapter six. The ב means "in," the ו is a token of Jehovah, the ו is the token of the Holy Ghost, and אל is short for Elohim. Thus *vouel*

133

(vowel) means "in the Godhead" and *vou* (vow) means "in Jehovah and the Holy Ghost," a perfect word for a solemn promise made to God. This would also explain why the *owl*, a transliteration of the Hebrew cryptogram וואל, is a symbol of wisdom, for the solution of this cryptogram is the "Godhead." **The gist of all this is that there is a link between the Godhead and vowels: the Hebrew characters that serve as tokens of the Godhead are the vowels of the alphabet.**

It should be clear from the previous chapters what these tokens are: א is the first letter of Elohim and is the token of Elohim, as in the words *Borashes* (p. 70), *mina* (p. 73), *S(h)inai* (p. 68), *ai* (p. 68), *adieu* (p. 82), *vowel,* and *owl*; י is the first letter of Jehovah and is a token of Jehovah, as in the words *chaiim* (p. 99), *yad* (p. 121), *Borashes, Ushio* (p. 74), *adieu, Je suis* (p. 82), *Yodyod, Hawaii, Sawaii, Tama alii,* and *ii* (all on p. 78); ו (o) is a token of Jehovah, as in the terms *Zion* (p. 87), *zohar* (p. 88), *bechomosaiy* (p. 121), *shalom* (Jehovah is the Prince of Peace), *Ushio, (w)o*—the direct object particle with a quiescent *w* in Japanese (p. 73)—and the Japanese honorific *o, vowel, vow,* and *owl*; and ו is the token of the *Ruach* (Holy Ghost) in the words *Urim* (pp. 99–100), *Upharsin* (p. 73), *Ushio, adieu, quorum* (p. 93), *vowel, vow,* and *owl.* Notice that just as there are four tokens given in the temple, there are four tokens of the Godhead in the Hebrew alphabet.

Thus the vowels of the Hebrew alphabet are א (a), י (i), ו (o), and ו (u). This is a revolutionary concept because the Hebrew scholars do not consider the *aleph* or the *yod* to be vowels, nor do they consider the ו (o), and ו (u) to be the 23rd and 24th letters of the Hebrew alphabet respectively. Hebraists feel that the *vav* comprises the ו (o), and ו (u), yet the *vav* is the only letter in the Hebrew alphabet that the reader does not know how to pronounce without the *dagesh*: it can be a *v/w, o,* or *u* sound. A perfect example is *Orim* versus *Urim*—the words are not synonymous, and the placement of the *dagesh* is the only distinguishing *point.* If there were no vowels in the original Hebrew, the reader would not know how to pronounce אורים.

Another ideal example is the tetragrammaton יהוה or the name *Jehovah.* Hebraists believe that the *vav* in יהוה is not a vowel, and even so, they vacillate over whether it should be transliterated a *v* or a *w*—without the vowels of the present system, יהוה is pronounced *Yahweh,* but with those vowel assignments, it is *Jehovah.* But while the scholars are wavering on the *v* or the *w,* the ו (o) remains a token of Jehovah (see above), and therefore His name is actually spelled with the ו (o) rather than the ו (v/w). Consequently, His name should be pronounced *Yehoah* rather than Jehovah or Yahweh. In summation, the Jews are confused on the pronunciation of the Lord's name for three reasons: one, for centuries they did not say it for fear of taking His sacred name in vain; two, they do not know that the ו (o) is a token of Jehovah because they do not believe in a Godhead; if Elohim, Jehovah, and the *Ruach* were the same God, then why do they have different tokens? And three, because the ו (o) and the ו (v/w) are the same letter in their understanding of the alphabet, they really do not know how to pronounce a *vav* when they see it. This illustrates once again that there is a need for the ו (o), and ו (u) to be separate letters from the *vav*, and that the present system is flawed.

Further evidence that the proper spelling and pronunciation is *Yehoah* and not Jehovah or Yahweh, is in the meaning of His name: the *yod* means "He will be"; the first *heh* signifies "He is"; the second *heh* signifies "He was"; and only if the *vav* has a *dagesh* directly above it does it mean "He creates." Since truth is the knowledge of the past, present, and future (D&C 93:24), then *Yehoah* (יהוה), not Jehovah (יהוה), resounds that He is indeed the author of all truth. Moreover, since *Yehoah* has another title, "The Creator," it fits that His name is spelled with the ו (o) and not the ו (v/w). Other examples of this meaning of "creation" in the ו (o) are the words *bechomosaiy* (p. 121) which means "in life *created* by my death," and *Zion* (p. 87), which means "righteousness that Yehoah *creates* is faithful forever." Notice that both words have a ו and not a ו, and the *v/w* is silenced because of the *dagesh* directly above the *vav*.

Reverting to the proposition that the ו (o), and ו (u) are the 23rd and 24th letters of the Hebrew alphabet: perhaps the Godhead chose the sixth letter *vav* to make two other letters that are tokens of the Godhead because They created man on the sixth day and the *vav* resembles a human chromosome (ו) ; and also a nail. Moreover, the angle of the *vav* (120°) is the same angle that light makes when passing through the prismatic system of the Urim and Thummim (see glyphic on p. 4). Notice that the angle is divisible by 24, and three make a full circle, or the Godhead.

Lucifer's counter-spin on the *vav* lends further credence to this position: since the *vav* also depicts a serpent and serpents kill man (see p. 66), Lucifer used the serpent as his vehicle in the Garden of Eden, and mutated the וֹ (o) and the וּ (u) to create his token וֹ (*Wo*), which resembles a spitting cobra. This mutation by Satan also explains why the Hebrew grammarians do not know where to put the *dagesh* over the *vav*: when they saw וֹ and וּ, they assumed וֹ and וּ were the same, and so when they created the present vowel system, they placed the dot of the vowel *o* over the left-hand corner of the letter, in between the dots of וֹ (wo) and וֹ (o). (See Mansoor's *Biblical Hebrew*, vol. 1:30.) Satan loves the confusion, because the true meanings and pronunciations of certain words get muddled, and sometimes there is no clear distinction between sacred and satanic terminologies. The camouflage is enhanced by Santa, a dyslexic form of Satan, saying *Ho Ho Ho,* which means "eat, drink, and be merry," instead of *Wo Wo Wo,* to warn us of Satan.

The truth is that the Godhead silenced the serpent (*Wo*) with the *dagesh* directly above (o) or in the middle (u) of the *vav*, and similitudes of this are the brazen serpent (Num. 21:9), and Aaron's rod, which became a serpent and ate all of Pharaoh's serpents (Ex. 7:12). Lucifer however is relentless, and continued to twist the story by creating with four *vavs* a swastika—an emblem of *luck*, and the Nazi logo.

Also corroborating this stance on the וֹ (o), and וּ (u) are the parallels between the human genome and the alphabet. Even as there is no life without genes, there is no language without letters, and it may be more than happenstance that there are the same number of letters (22) in the standard Hebrew alphabet as there are different human autosomes (the chromosomes other than the sex chromosomes). If the ו (o), and ו (u) indeed were the 23rd and 24th letters, they would correspond to the Y and X chromosomes respectively. Moreover, just as there are four bases in DNA arranged in groups of three called *codons*, the Hebrew alphabet has four tokens (vowels) of the Godhead comprising three Gods. What perfect correlations—without DNA, vowels, or the Godhead, there would be no life (see p. 131)—and they do not stop here.

One of the four DNA bases—thymine—is found exclusively in DNA not RNA, while the other bases are common to both DNA and RNA. Therefore DNA and the nucleus of the cell are a similitude of celestial glory since Elohim (א) can only live on a celestial sphere. RNA and the cytoplasm are a similitude of terrestrial glory since *Yehoah* and the *Ruach* can reside there, and the *heh* (ה) in *Yehoah* corresponds to the uridine base in RNA that is substituted for the thymine in DNA. Thus the *heh* (ה) is a half-token of the Godhead and a pseudo-vowel of the Hebrew alphabet. Indeed, many of the names in the stick of Judah (Abraham, Sarah, Jeremiah, Methuselah, Micah, Elijah, Isaiah, etc.) and the stick of Joseph (Moronihah, Ammonihah, Cumenihah, Limhah, and Zemnarihah) have "*h*"s branded in them from *Yehoah*—in fact, the latter names have both "*h*"s from *Yehoah*. It is sort of a cultural distinction that the Nephites grafted both "*h*"s from *Yehoah* while the ancient Israelites used only one.

As for pseudo-vowels, the *heh* is sometimes transliterated as an *e* in the English—for example, aleph (a), beth (b), gimel (c), daleth (d), *heh* (e). The ﬠ (as in *Eber*) is also a pseudo-vowel since it too is sometimes transliterated an *e* in the English. This might help to explain why the Hebraists who revivified the language concluded that there were no vowels in the Hebrew alphabet because they knew that the *heh* (ה) and the *ayin* (ﬠ) are really consonants regardless of their transliterations.

To complete the analogy between *three degrees of glory* and genetics: proteins and the extracellular space typify telestial glory, and mutated genes, defective proteins, and waste products typify hell or outer darkness. This also implies that what makes us "mortal" is that proteins directly control our physical bodies, the prime example being that the protein *hemoglobin* is the main constituent of blood—a telestial trademark (Lev. 17:11). Moreover, in the millennium, since we will be living on a terrestrial sphere, RNA may directly control our bodily functions, which would render our cells self-sufficient and the circulatory system vestigial. Is it possible that in the transfigured state, the cells of the human body become self-sufficient and this is how Moses, Elijah, and Jesus survived forty-day fasts?

Finally, the secret to the "fallen state" may lie in the sex chromosomes: they are paired up in men even though they are different chromosomes, and women are "missing" the 23rd (*Y*) chromosome. Perhaps we have mutated celestial sex chromosomes, just as the ו (wo) is a mutated ו (o), and ו (u) that correspond to those celestial sex chromosomes which contain celestial DNA. Once again, there is more to *wo* than woe.

Let's explore further the implications of the *Y* chromosome: "Therefore, the Lord Himself shall give you a *sign*: Behold, a *virgin* shall conceive, and bear a *son*" (Isa. 7:14). The Hebrew rendition uses the word אות for *sign*, and says *ha-almah* meaning "the virgin," not "a virgin." The notion that *ha-almah* does not connote an unspotted virgin is silly because her conception would no longer be a sign (miracle). אות is a cryptogram meaning *Yehoah* twice: the ו is a token of *Yehoah,* as is the את since *Yehoah* is *Alpha and Omega, the beginning and the end.* It is highly significant that the Lord used the word אות when he could have used the word *nes*, the demotic word for "miracle," or *temah*, the word for "miracle" that has a *heh* in it from *Yehoah.* When the Lord revealed to Isaiah His future Immaculate Conception, He chose the word אות because of the double *Yehoah* (also a double objective case since *et* and *o* are the direct object particles in Hebrew and Japanese respectively—see pp. 72–73) **including the ו**, which correlates with the *Y* chromosome. You see, the full miracle in the Immaculate Conception was that a virgin conceived a son, since in our day virgins can conceive daughters but not sons with cloning technology. Therefore, there was at least one distinguishing feature that separated *Yehoah* from the rest of the males on this planet: He had Elohim's *Y* chromosome, or the ו (o) in Elohim—yes, Elohim may have originally been spelled with an ו (o). It fits that Elohim would have three of the tokens of the Godhead in His name, Jehovah would have two, and the Holy Ghost one. Elohim gave two of

His tokens to His Only Begotten Son, but He saved the *aleph* for only Himself since *aleph* is the first letter of the alphabet and represents the number *one* and Elohim is number one in the Universe.

The number 24 is significant for reasons other than the alphabet and the human genome: 24 patriarchs from Adam to Ephraim; 24 elders surrounding the throne of God (Rev. 4); two sets of twelve apostles, one for the land of Judah, and one for the land of Joseph; 24 teachers in a quorum of teachers and 48 priests in a priests' quorum corresponding to the celestial diploid (the mortal diploid has 46 chromosomes), and 96 elders in an elders' quorum corresponding to the replicated celestial diploid; 24 essential organic nutrients for the human body—nine amino acids, two fatty acids, and 13 vitamins (Harrison's *Principles of Internal Medicine*); 24 hours in a day; lastly, Egyptian, the oldest writing ever discovered by modern man, had a 24-letter alphabet (Hugh Nibley's *Temple and Cosmos*, p. 480), the average of a 22-letter standard Hebrew alphabet and a 26-letter English alphabet.

It is also crucial to discuss the origin of the *dagesh* in the current vowel system. The truth is that grammarians knew to incorporate it because it was indeed extant in the original Hebrew, **but only as a pointer to sacred things**. (This is why only the *vav* with a *dagesh* is a token of the Godhead.) The four tokens given in the temple are a clue to this usage: **they each have a *dagesh* in them**. There would be no doubt of the meaning of *Borashes,* which is either "in the beginning" or "in the Godhead and God's obedient descendants" if an ו (u) were inserted making *Berushes*: now it unquestionably has the second meaning because the *ru* can only come from *Ruach* since the ו is the token of the *Ruach*, and besides, **the *dagesh* points to the sacred meaning**. The insertion of the ו in *Borashes* would also explain where the names *Bruce, Rusch,* and *Russia* originated. Moreover, there would be no doubt to the meaning of the copula *and* if there were a *dagesh* in it rendering an *oo* pronunciation (see p. 74). This grammatical usage would also explain why there is a *dagesh* in כהן (*cohen*), which means "priest of Aaron," and two in כהן גדול meaning "high priest." Or why תמה means *miracle*, but without the *dagesh*, it means *magic*. In the Adamic language, if *"gadol"* were not used in a sacred context, it would be pronounced *gadval* because there would be no *dagesh* above the *vav*. Another example is the word *shalom*.

In summation, five revolutionary conclusions have been drawn in this chapter: one, that the four characters of the Hebrew alphabet serving as tokens of the Godhead are the vowels of the Hebrew alphabet, and correspond to the four DNA bases and the four tokens in the temple; two, that the *dagesh* (·) indeed did exist in the original Hebrew or the Adamic language, but its exclusive use was to point to something sacred; three, that Jehovah should really be spelled with an ו and pronounced *Yehoah*; four, that there are the same number of letters in the Hebrew alphabet as there are different human chromosomes, the 23rd letter (ו)and the 24th letter (ו) correspond to the *Y* and *X* chromosomes respectively; and five, that the DNA codon is a similitude of the Godhead.

129
Mouth 5, 52
Murder 29, 32, 51
Museum of the Lord 81
Mysteries of God 3, 13, 39,
49, 50, 69, 101, 104

N

Naomi(Marah) 120
Natural Man 28, 36, 48,
57, 58
Nauvoo 53, 85
Nazi 124
Nephi 11, 29, 36, 83, 89
Nevada 85
New Name 102, 120, 121
New Test. Hist. 90, 91
Newton 11
Nibley, Hugh 14, 131, 140
Nimiety 25
Noah 54, 72, 75, 81, 88,
89, 92, 97, 110, 112,
114–116, 127
Numerator 49

O

O (ỉ) 4, 5, 18, 73, 87,
133–142
Obesity 31, 60
Omega 71, 73, 82, 83
One Eternal Round 4, 5, 32,
100–101
Ondi 88
Opposition 10, 11, 20, 21,
34-36, 47, 60

Oracle 5
Oregon 85
Orient 10
Owl 134

P

Palestine 80
Palmyra, N.Y. 76
Passover 72, 90, 114, 118,
119, 123, 124
Patience 3, 25, 28, 38, 50, 62
Patriarchal Blessing 11
Patriarchal Order 67, 72,
115, 117, 130, 139
Patten, G.S. 33
Paul 11, 12, 17, 21, 25, 34,
37–43, 116, 120
Pavlov 48
Pe Le El 5, 120
Peace 6, 19, 28, 30, 58, 59
Perish 19
Persia 73, 74
Peter 13, 20, 42, 110, 114,
116, 120
Phineas 3, 29, 101
Plagues 55, 63
Polygamy 30
Polynesia 78
Ponce De Leon 65
Poor in Spirit 58, 59
Prayer 23, 24, 27
Prayer (Cohen) 6, 109
Prayer (Serenity) 59
Pre-Earth Life 50
Pregnancy 51

151

United Order 54
Upharsin 73
Urim 3, 5, 14, 38, 39, 45, 49, 81, 91–103, 134, 135, 140
Uri Tzvi Sr. (Rabbi) 3
Ushio 74, 134
Utah 31, 51, 85

V

Vav (ו) 5, 44–46, 74, 133–137, 139–142
Veil 42, 120
Vision, Spiritual 5, 7, 9, 13, 16, 19, 23, 32
Vowels 4, 5, 18, 133–142

W

Washington D.C. 126
White 28, 35
Whitehead, A.N. 59
Wine 89-90
Witch of Endor 76
Wo, Wo, Wo 4, 45, 46, 82, 136, 137, 139
Word of Wisdom 65, 90
Worldwide Web (WWW) 44, 45

Y

Yayin 83
Yehoah 135–138, 140–142
Yiddish 14, 82, 130
Yizkor 126
Yod 70, 82, 87
Yod, Tau 70

Yod Yod (יי) 78, 94, 99
Yom Bechomosai 121, 125, 134, 136
Yom Kippur (Day of Atonement) 2, 95, 98, 108, 128, 129
Young, Brigham 33

Z

Zacharias 3, 95, 96, 104, 125
Zadok 3, 95
Zechariah 3, 129
Zenos 81
Zimri 29
Zion 85, 87–89, 124, 134, 136
Zipporah 31
Zohar 88, 134